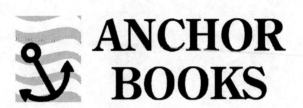
ANCHOR
BOOKS

POETS' PRIDE IN THE UK

Edited by

Heather Killingray

First published in Great Britain in 1998 by
ANCHOR BOOKS
1-2 Wainman Road, Woodston,
Peterborough, PE2 7BU
Telephone (01733) 230761

HB ISBN 1 85930 569 5
SB ISBN 1 85930 564 4

FOREWORD

Anchor Books is a small press, established in 1992, with the aim of promoting readable poetry to as wide an audience as possible.

We hope to establish an outlet for writers of poetry who may have struggled to see their work in print.

The poems presented here have been selected from many entries. Editing proved to be a difficult task and as the Editor, the final selection was mine.

Poets' Pride In The UK is a compilation of poetry which has been assembled using the work of poets from all over the United Kingdom.

The poems vary in style and content, ranging from what they like about their home town/city to pleasant memories they have about a particular aspect of life whilst living in their home town/city.

Each poem in this collection is unique and shows the reader, how proud they are to live in the United Kingdom.

An inspirational collection for one and all to read time and time again.

I trust this selection will delight and please the authors and all those who enjoy reading poetry.

Heather Killingray
Editor

CONTENTS

WHISPERING STONES

Long stones, standing stones, whispering stones.
In circles some stand in sombre stance
Each to an ancestor, aeons gone,
Each when sons and descendants stood
When at dawn they vowed to the rising sun.

And upon the stunted windswept heath
Winds shrieking their eerie wail,
Cairn Kenidzhek rises high,
Rearing darkly, crag on crag,
Against the bleak and empty sky.

Northward there stretches the even plain
And the moors where the Cornu-Briton
Hunted the boar and the savage segh,
Their segh-dogs racing and giving tongue
As they hurled themselves upon their prey.

From an ancient village, large stones pave the way
To the fortification of Castle Chun
On the summit looking over the moor,
Protected by ditch and broad wide fosse
And outer wall of five span or more.

And there on the hillside beneath the castle,
A long stone, standing stone, whispering stone,
A Men Scryfa - a stone to revere,
Which is written - 'Rialobran, Cunoval Fil' -
Rialobran, son of Cunoval lies here.

Esme Francis

TRAMS

'Trams, what were they?' a little child asked
A teacher at school one day
It was like a train but not as big
It looked like a bus but ran on a rail
One was above and the other in the road
Were very noisy and weren't any good.
Ran on iron wheels and made such a noise
The driver stood up to drive with such poise.
It cost a halfpenny to go into town.
And to the beach if a penny you found
For fifty years they travelled the land
Until taken over by the bus better and grand
Here in Sunderland a special tram of lights
When switched on was such an amazing sight
From the Roker cafe to Seaburn Camp
You could travel along and see the lights
But on Tunstall Hill in 1954
The tramcar was to know its fate.
On bonfire night, 6 in all went up
In a blaze of glory people loved or did hate.

Ray T Duncan

UNTITLED

We talk about the jobs that have gone
How the kids are doing at school
What's on the telly
Being down the pub, playing pool

We muddle on the best we can
Walking on our own street
Coping when times are bad
We empathise with those we meet

They can take away our futures
Plunge us into an abyss
But they can't take what we will miss
Can't take away what we hold dear
And that's our pride of the Tyne and Wear

Maria Waters

MAWNAN SMITH - OUR VILLAGE

Nestled amid rolling hills, a short walk away from thecoast
Lies the village of Mawnan Smith, of which we proudly boast
Three churches and a chapel, to offer peace and quiet
While the Red Lion Inn serves food and drink to make you rue the diet
Three general stores to meet your needs with wares too vast to mention
At the Post office you could win the lottery, or just go and draw your
pension
We have, of course, a butcher, a purveyor of fine meat
A restaurant that will thrill you with a first class gourmet treat
To browse around our 'Hammer and Hoe' folk come from near and far
And ample room in the square if you wish to park your car
Our hairdresser will delight you with dexterity and skills
A surgery three times a week where you can get your pills
At 'Electric's' shop you can renew a fuse or buy an electric fire
We also have a fashion shop, full of ladies fine attire
Two banks and a house agent, if your house you wish to sell
A really excellent garage, if your car's not going so well
There is, of course, the primary school for those not in their teens
And don't forget our bowling club with its two, three rink greens
Last, but by no means least, we have our memorial ball
Where something is happening all the time and enjoyed by one and all
Mawnan Smith is full of life, a very lovely village
To live here and meet the folk, is really quite a privilege

Les Parsons

CORNWALL, (AS I SEE IT)

Come with me to Cornwall, so much beauty you will find,
A county with many aspects, of a rich and varied kind.
Hear the tales of long ago, of intrigue and of mystery,
Pixies, ghosts and pirates, and all its ancient history.

See the shaggy highland cattle, on the misty windswept moors,
Miles of boggy grassland, surround the rugged tors.
A truly wild and barren place, but home to sheep and horse,
Scarce a tree will grow there, only heath and gorse.

Wander down the country lanes, so narrow and so winding,
Stone hedges built on either side, with only soil for binding,
Admire the flowers that grow there, the ferns and mosses too,
A joy for all who see them, when spring comes forth anew.

Watch the busy farmer, he hardly ever stops,
A job for every season, tending animals and crops.
Go to town on market day, and hear the auction cry.
Or listen to the dialect, as the crowds pass by.

Gaze up at huge white mountains, of waste from china clay,
Glistening in the sunlight, and growing higher every day.
Sent to countries far and wide, by road and by the sea,
It's Cornwall's largest export, and used in mill and pottery.

Remember all the miners, when you see an ivy covered stack,
Long hours or working underground, where it's cold and damp
and black
Brave men in constant danger, from flood or caving in,
Seldom seeing light of day, in their search for tin.

Explore the jagged coastline, with surging foaming seas,
Feel the soft and golden sand, and the warm and salty breeze.
Visit little harbour towns, with seagulls on the wing,
Full of noise and bustle, and fisherman that sing.

Join the celebrations, on Helston flora day,
Couples visit houses, as they dance along the way.
Remember Padstow hobby horse, in the month of May,
Welcoming the start of summer and driving winter far away.

Watch the morris dancers, performing in the street,
Dressed in fancy costumes, with bells upon their feet.
Listen to the local bands, making music all around,
At all the fetes and carnivals, that's where they'll be found.

Now sit upon the rocky slopes, as you reach Land's End,
And think of all her beauty, before you homeward wend.
Take one last look at Cornwall, the life, the sea, the moor,
And listen to the thunder, of the great Atlantic's roar.

J M Philp

PORTRAIT OF YORKSHIRE

County of broad acres, rolling moors and lonely fells,
Great cities, villages of stone, lovely peaceful dales.
Seaside towns, dramatic cliffs, from Whitby to Flamborough Head,
Market towns and hamlets some deserted now, and dead.
York with its ancient walls and Minster, where the Vikings used
                                                    to dwell,
Mill shops in towns where wool was king, with varied wares to sell.
Haworth has its cobbled streets, where the Brontes wrote their tales,
There are lakes and dams, and reservoirs, where folk go fishing,
                                                    and for sails.
Still some mills, though fewer now, where worsted cloth is made,
Fields full of flowers, and bluebell woods where, as kids, we played.
A sporting county, games for all, cricket, football, mountain biking,
To suit all tastes and pockets, from flying down to hiking!
Our county has almost everything, as any Yorkshireman will tell,
The largest county in the land - and we think, the best, as well!

Kathleen Adams

WEARSIDE'S HISTORY

Wearside, it does house so much, well steeped in history
It started ages long ago, this great flowing story
Commencing in the cold North Sea, Wear winds its pathway through
And cuts the city of Sunderland so neatly in two.

It moves on in its glory, from sea through shore it flows
Holding in many a secret, that only water knows
Monkwearmouth and to Deptford, then Hylton and Cox Green
From our great Penshaw monument, its glory can still be seen

Meandering to Chester-le-Street, in its way no dam
Onward still to county home, historic old Durham
Passing Durham Castle and also Durham Cathedral
Before making its countryside stop, in our most beautiful Weardale

This Wear it's seen the launch of ships, gliding from their birth
And guided people on their way, rowing its banks in mirth
This Wear has housed the dockyards too, where food's brought in to eat
And seen so many celebrate, in watering holes they'd meet

Our Wearside it provides for all, for work as well as play
From Weardale back to Wearmouth, it's set for sure, to stay
For all of those who see her flow and those who live nearby
She'll be there for all time, for all, beneath the Lord's own sky

Paul Christie

MY CITY

Students of the world pass by every day
to Sunderland University they make their way
colourful and eager they chatter away
who will be what at the end of their stay
Industrialist, tycoons, who can say.
A future Prime Minister could pass this way.

Graduation day is a sea of gowns
clutching diplomas relieved and proud
can't wait to do well and show the world
all you have learned, the pride that I feel
as I watch you leave
Sunderland, my city, I'm so proud of thee.

Margaret Overy

CORNISH PRIDE

As I stand here once more
on this great Cornish shore,
and I watch the white surf and the sea,
I am pleased with it all
as I hear the gulls call
We are free! We are free! We are free,

You are mad, Cornishman, if you ever plan
to leave home for material gain,
for it's all at your door
as you stand on this shore
don't look elsewhere, or you'll look in vain.

I met a young man, from a far distant land
with his wet suit and surf board so fine.
He said often I've roamed
but I'd never leave my home
if this part of the world was all mine.

So be proud of your land
raise your flag, make your stand,
and let nothing tempt you to stray.
As you repeat your great call
'One and all! One and all!'
in the true Celtic, Cornish way.

Gerry Concah

LEICESTERSHIRE

We cannot boast of lofty mountains
Rolling downs or windswept moors -
Valleys deep or mighty forests -
Craggy cliffs or sandy shores.
We have a green and pleasant landscape -
Hills that have stood the test of time -
Bradgate with its rugged splendour
and Swithland woods where bluebells chime.
We have our share of parks and gardens -
Stately homes that we can view,
winding lanes where we can wander
far from all the cry and hue.
Villages and tiny hamlets
spread out like a patchwork quilt -
A famous road we call the Fosse Way
which long ago the Romans built.
Climb to the top of Beacon Hill
on a calm and quiet day -
Look out over Leicestershire
and you'll not question why you stay.

Constance Smith

PAUSE FOR THOUGHT IN SUNDERLAND

Do you remember when shipyards were booming?
Thompson's, Pickersgill's, and Doxford's too?
Employing thousands of men and women
Could one of them have been you?

Do you remember when coalfields were stacked high?
Ryhope, Silksworth, Monkwearmouth, to name but a few?
Miners, all dirty with callused hands,
and pit ponies working there too?

Do you remember the Strand, Blacketts?
And Liverpool House gracing High Street?
And Binns, the pride of Fawcett Street?
All big stores in their prime,
Have now disappeared through time.

Do you remember when jobs were not hard to find,
In the places I've mentioned,
Now left far behind?

John Heads

HERE'S TO THE FUTURE - TYNE & WEAR

From the backbone of Old England
To the tangy, restless sea,
Twin rivers deep and flowing
Have claimed this land for me.

Its vistas ever changing
With something new each dawn,
Have gladdened every heartbeat
Since the day that I was born.

Mighty ships were spawned there,
On the rivers' ebb and flood
And coal and glass and copperas
Are surely in my blood.

I've watched the mighty furnace
With sweat upon my brow,
On the riverside in falling soot.
A linnet sings there now.

We've a great and glorious past.
I know, I'm very proud.
But we've an even greater future.
Tell the world, shout it loud!

Dennis Bulmer

PROGRESS

Look what they've gone and done to our town
They've torn the old market and cinema down
Concrete high rises they've put in their place
No longer the stalls of perfume and lace.
The slow moving pace of life as we knew
Is replaced by a race and a long winding queue
Gone are the shops with the personal touch
The greed for quick profits took over so much.
The picture house too, has gone now today
They've built a big store and a pub in the way
They took down the Kid's park and locked up the gate
To build the civic centre in the shape of an eight.
No longer needed, we lost the town hall
Creating the space for a new shopping mall
The hotel was grand, by nature and name
Mindless destruction, to add to the shame.
The quaint little streets where we used to walk
Destroyed to make way for a multi car park
The riverside bank where the industry lay
Turned into flats where the privileged play.
They've taken our airfield which stood on green land
Made it a workshop for cars made by hand
Cutting new roads through our woodland and field
Disturbing the wildlife and making it yield.
The heavy approach of the governing hand
Sometimes just doesn't go quite as it's planned
The changes should be for the good of us all
Hear our opinions, don't make us feel small.

P Jeffrey

LEICESTERSHIRE THE HEART OF ENGLAND

Borders carved by byways, clear wandering streams,
England's heart shaped county, cardi-fitly placed.
Or vulpine headed outline, Quorn hunt chased -
Over rolling Melton's hills, rich pink teams.
Melton pies, tastes of Leicester - Stilton cheese -
Enjoyed in country inns, with Langham beer.
Eight reservoirs are fished before they freeze.
Bright sails skim by as yachtsmen-leaning steer.
Its highest point on lofty Bardon Hill
Commands fine views to county's farthest edge.
Facing east over site of Woodhouse mill,
No earthly soil as high, till Urals ledge.
St Bernard's monastery, active and serene.
Ancient Gracedieu ruins no way demean.

Markfield's grey granite, Groby's greenish tone.
Red rocks of Mount Sorrel, Swithland grey slate.
Reinforced with limestone, their strength create,
Eastern ironstone churches, storm weather blown.
Forests rugged beauty, sunsets unique.
Brick built villages, undulating clay lands.
Slow willow fringed streams, Soar to the Wreake.
Unspoiled hamlets, roofed by skilled hands.
Cossington's Soar suits Constable or Turner.
Foxton locks lift barges seventy feet high.
Footpaths for skilled hikers, flat for the learner.
Eyebrook remembers the Dambusters fly.
Battlefields, the Leicesters, mining, bells - its sheep.
Proud county - proud workers - proud standards keep.

Derek E Akers

SUMMER NIGHTS IN BITTESWELL

Barbecue odours drift across the hedge,
babies go reluctantly, tearfully, up to bed;
practice bells are silent at last
and ringers snug in the Oak.

In the magic mushroom cricket field
the last over is finally over,
teenagers hang out noisily on the green,
cats melt away into the night unseen.

The wind drops, everything is still;
evening primroses begin mysteriously
to unfold their beauty, one by one,
under the steadily rising, confident moon.

A solitary hedgehog shuffles through the bushes,
intent on scraps from the cats' Whiskas.
Frenzied frogs leap higher and higher,
baby rabbits play follow my leader.

Rapacious snails make their nightly assaults
on vulnerable trailing petunias;
later the fox patrols his territory
while elderly insomniacs endlessly brew tea.

Percy the peacock heralds the dawn
and a refugee family of ducks arrives
to waddle about, commandeer the lawn
and make an inconvenient mess.

Nocturnal jaunts accomplished, the cats return;
milk bottles clink and a bike creaks
up the garden path - a paper flops
on to the parquet. Another day has begun.

Pat Foster

MARKET HARBOROUGH IN LEICESTERSHIRE

My nearest town is cosy Market Harborough,
Which I visit nearly every day.
It has all my needs and is pleasant,
And I meet many friends along the way.

The Welland River flows through,
It has moorhens and ducks.
And at last, our High Street,
Has less and less trucks.

Shops, there are many with specials,
As Gilberts and Emerson and West.
The choice is most varied,
For you to search for the best.

The church in the centre
The old grammar school - a gem.
The theatre is thriving,
It's for us, you and them.

It has its own leisure centre,
A golf course of note.
And hostelries galore,
To push out the boat.

It's endearing is Harborough,
With history quite old.
There are many true Harborians,
With tales to be told.

So a message to all,
To keep our town alive.
In this way we prosper,
We shop and we thrive.

Colin Fraser

LEICESTERSHIRE

In Leicester's green and lovely shire,
The rolling pastures gently flow,
Enriched by many a noble spire
From very earth which seems to grow.

The wooded copse, the winding lane,
The tinkling stream whose music sings
Of happiness, and hope again
Of peace, and love, and joyful things.

The soaring birds attain the sky,
These winged choirs who fly so free,
Their anthem swells and rises high
From choir stall set on lofty tree.

Beneath, the patient cattle stand
In hedgerowed fields of verdant green,
While Leicester's far famed sheep, a band
Of white spread o'er this sylvan scene.

There lies an ancient Manor House
In stately park-land, setting meet,
While here a cottage nestles close,
Secure in sweetly flowered retreat.

No mountain range, no lofty peaks
Have we to show in Leicester's land,
But he who gentler beauty seeks
May find it here on every hand.

For Leicestershire is England's heart,
In place and form 'tis plain to see,
And Leicestershire has played its part,
And will to all eternity.

Bernard Laughton

THANKS FOR THE MEMORY

The Leicester I knew of long ago,
With horse-drawn cart and rattling tram,
of cobbled streets and lamplight man.

Walking to school along Bird Cage Walk,
potato picking, instead of sport.
The bobby on his box directing the flow,
from Gallowtree Gate to Halford Street,
or around the Tower
where we've now got seats.

Or a trip to the market on a Saturday night,
hot peas near the Saracen's Head while my dad had a pint.
Then on to Joblins to buy a few sweets,
before going to the Palace for our Saturday treat,
to sit in The Gods and watch the show
or drop sweet wrappers on the crowd below.

On the nights when the searchlights scanned the sky
as German bombers throbbed up high,
reports from abroad of a desert victory
and American troops in our fair city.

Queuing for hot dogs in Humberstone Gate,
young men in khaki, young men in blue,
even the Italians and Germans came too.
They put them in a camp on Shady Lane, for a time,
the road to Evington didn't seem quite the same.
Dancing round the Tower on Victory Night,
to me, really was a great delight.

Now the Leicester that I knew has nearly gone . . .
but the memories are there and they'll linger on.

G Clarke

LEICESTERSHIRE CAT

I come from a long line of country cats
It used to be fields and farms
And my ancestors controlled the mice and rats
But now it's shops - to supply my feed and anything else I might need

Every day I have little to do, if wet I've a choice of two
Places to visit. Both warm and bright. Just which scent
Does my nose prefer soap powder or shampoo?
Friends always open the doors for me to go through.

I quite like the hum of the dryers and from here
I can keep my eye on the fish shop which opens at noon
I fancy a bit of fish for lunch but don't want to get there too soon
It doesn't do to look too eager, but mustn't nod off and be too late.

If it's a hot summer day I just laze on the grass
And watch the people and cars as they pass
Cars must not stop or they will get a ticket
Will I get one if I sit on the road? If so, where will they stick it?

I wear evening dress with pride, white bib and spats
As up the road I stroll - Will the cake shop have a sausage roll?
I walk on the yellow line - it's smooth to my feet
I rather fancy an eclair - I wonder if they will have one to spare.

M E Holmes

DAYS GONE BY

She sits on the banks of the River Wear
  Thinking of days gone by,
Of the days that she spent, having so much fun,
  To think of them makes her cry.

Remembering back to the days she was young
  when she laughed and cried and played.
Remembering back to the good old days
  her memories will never fade.

The Garths have gone, the home she knew
   Her granny, her mother, her Aunt Mary too.
St Peter's Church she can see so clearly
   is all that's left of the days she holds dearly

Her son was born, her daughter too,
   in the house in the Garths that she once knew.
With sorrow and pain, she sits by the Wear
   Remembering the days that she'll always hold dear.

Jeanette Cheal

I LOVE THE WAY

I love the way you talk
- the gentle, soft undulation
            of your words
- your native tongue in the syntax
            'It's me, it is!'

I love your friendliness
- your interest in people
- your natural curiosity
            about the who, what, where and when!
            Always time to say 'Hello.'

Be proud!
-of your roots deep in this Celtic soil

Be proud!
-of your identity
- rich and definable

Be proud
-of your people
- warm and strong.

Barbara Conneely

JUBILATE

(Dedicated to the Ammanford Choral Society on celebrating its Golden Jubilee in 1997)

After patient restoration and a sense of dedication
The Choir of blending voices has been heard;
With rhythmic hands aloft and no energy ever stopped,
The conductor's discipline has kept them stirred.

Complete with orchestration and a fiery imagination
The soloists have led them from the past,
Using Bible-themes dramatic and arias operatic,
Providing many memories that will last.

The musical notation and the visual stimulation,
As the changing moods have ever been portrayed,
Have gone from strength to strength along five decades length
And justly earned this present accolade.

With a sense of exultation after a well-deserved ovation,
This tribute to the Choir I now pay.
May the warmest acclamation and a sense of jubilation
Be truly theirs for many a livelong day.

Yvonne Watkin-Rees

THERE IS A DUTY

Sing a song of Rutland,
Sing a song of county,
Of rolling hills and distant greens
And sing the song of bounty.

Watch birds wheeling free in air,
Sniff the scent of wood-burning smoke
But let us all take care,
We're not part of the careless folk,

Who close eyes on the passing scene,
Ignore pollution and the warming earth,
Forget we inherited the past
And must hand on to future birth.

Shall we leave behind a desert
Where poisoned clouds hold sway
To our children and their children
When we have passed away?

L J Green

RETURNING

Tortoiseshell patchwork over forest green hills,
Dark clouds languor on the sea spray wind.
Bitter the ozone, heavy and strong,
That lies on the land of the storm to come.
White crested waves take on Pegasus wings,
Rolling on softly the sea song sings.
Deepening shadows over turbulent dreams,
Magenta the waters of the swift flowing streams.
Full moon rises as storm clouds build,
Suns last rays now the air be still.
Swallows here swoop and seagulls do cry,
Listen, faint splash as silver scales fly.
Fine mist dances on a young girl's face
As she wanders streets of crosspatched lace.
Rain hangs waiting high overhead,
Each cloud edged by a black silk thread.
Cooling the breeze on her dampened face,
Is it the salt of the sea she tastes?
Deep in this land feel the song so sweet
Found is the peace she has come to seek.

Karen

THE ELAN VALLEY

It's a long time since I've been there where we used to go alone,
    We walked and talked together and spent our nights at home.
I remember birds and flowers, little lambs upon the hill.
    The warmth of summer evenings, and lakes that lie so still.
I love the Elan Valley, and I love the water too,
    Windcalls and waterfalls remind me of you.

There's an emptiness inside me like I've never known before
    I often miss the good times, how could I ask for more.
Well I've been across the water and I've been in heaven too
    How could I e'er forget those heavenly times I spent with you.
I love the Elan Valley, and I love the water too,
    Windcalls and waterfalls remind me of you.

Well, I can't go on without you so no longer will I roam.
    The wind across the valley keeps calling me back home
Once again we'll walk together where those dams so tall they stand,
    I know of nothing that compares with this, my father's land.
I love the Elan Valley, and I love the water too,
    Windcalls and waterfalls remind me of you.

Clive Jones

PARTS OF LEICESTER

Beacon Hill, Swithland Woods
Such beautiful countryside
At Beacon Hill you can see
Miles and miles of Leicestershire.

Stroll through the woods at Swithland
Bluebells bright can be seen
Birds do sing up in the trees
Beneath those leafy awnings.

Victoria Park with De Montfort Hall
Is a popular place for folks to call
Concerts and artists do come there
For us to see, for us to share.

Spinney Hill and other fine parks
For children to play, for fairs to alight
Different stalls and food stalls aplenty
Do take place occasionally.

Sheila Wall

MEN OF YORKSHIRE

There's nowt so queer as folk they say
But Yorkshire man is particular in his way
Football, rugby and Yorkshire cricket
He likes all sports, no sticky wickets
He likes his tea and boiled ham
Curries, fish and chips and even spam (fried)
Thick in t'arm and strong in t'ead
Full of pud and drip and bread
And being Yorkshire born and bred
Upon his pint a decent head
Meat and veg and Barnsley chops
He will work until he drops
And racing pigeons our especial tyke
Will only swear by saying 'On yer bike'
And calling all his men friends' love
He reminds me of our Lord above

But if you can't fill his tum
It's 'Ee by gum' and home to Mum!

Paul Wright

THAT OLD OAK TREE OF CARMARTHEN TOWN

Merlin was born to this ancient town
And would ponder beneath the branches of,
That old oak tree of Carmarthen town.

It was born of a time
When magic did flow,
That old oak tree of Carmarthen town.

The history books all say
That he loved the solitude of,
That old oak tree of Carmarthen town.

His love was so strong
This prophecy he laid on,
That old oak tree of Carmarthen town.

I'll spare you your town
If you'll spare it for me,
That old oak tree of Carmarthen town.

So old had it grown
And so weary and sad,
That old oak tree of Carmarthen town.

How lonely it stood
In this road by itself,
That old oak tree of Carmarthen town.

Its branches all broken
And withered away,
That old oak tree of Carmarthen town.

They pulled it down
Just a short while ago,
That old oak tree of Carmarthen town.

Though the tree has now gone
Its tales will live on,
That old oak tree of Carmarthen town.

Michael Keddie

LOUGHBOROUGH FAIR

There's a cold nip in the damp November air
As my love and I roam round the fair
Weird and wonderful sights all round,
Blaring music all over the ground,
Barkers shouting to sell their wares,
Three darts below twenty to win a brown bear
To cover a number, roll pennies down,
To win a pink elephant, or a sad looking clown,
Tension, excitement, as the big wheel goes round
Shrieking laughter, raucous sound,
Out from a tub, wound on a long stick
Pink sticky candyfloss, ready to lick
Children tugging at coat sleeves 'Toffee apple, Dad, please'
Coconuts topple into sawdust below
Pleases a youth who has just aimed a throw.
Paintings on roundabouts in garish hues
Full bosomed ladies plump and fat,
Looking contented like purring cats
Hair of yellow, cheeks rosy red
Lips of carmine and eyes violet blue
These creatures so fair, painted by whom
Rembrandt, Lautrec, Van Gogh - I think not
I look, I ponder and then we walk off.

Elsie Squires

GARDEN

Look at me the colours say,
from pale pink to deep purple here I lay.
The rockery has no chance to show
its crystal head,
as the blanket of aubretia makes its bed.

Come bend and gaze upon my
glorious crown,
as the lily floats in her royal gown.

Water shudders and broken silver glints
reflecting the summer floral tints.

My home is here beneath the waters,
staring eye of the frog never falters.
A visitor with rainbow gossamer wings
darts overhead then to a plant she clings.

This garden speaks with her gentle tongue,
my beauty is forever young.

Poppy Ashfield

SEA MARSH - KIDWELLY

this is the low land
where low landers live
and the tidal reach
extends its fjord fingers
beyond the scrap of beach

only low landers know
the draw of mist and mud
where beast and fowl and fisherman
observe the monthly flood

fond air amidst the rain light
while all the world is mean
salt mixes with the given
low land, the in-between.

Jane Judge

RE-DISCOVER LEICESTER

Leicester - surprises at every turn,
A county of history and change,
Take a stroll around its new centre
Experience variety and range.

Architects have pondered hard,
Across the endless years,
Seek out some of our buildings,
They might move you to tears

But this is just a small piece,
Of a very much larger design,
Go and visit the Bradgate Park,
Any season -
It looks so divine.

And what of the past and its memories,
A county with such great romance,
Splendid tales of kings and their queens,
So cancel that day-trip to France!

Instead spend a day in your city,
You could be amazed what you'll find,
Rediscover a place you thought you knew well,
There's a chance it will broaden your mind.

Ashley Watson

HOME

Wales is a land of castles,
Of coal, of rugby, of song.
And when we're away for more than a day,
It's for the *green, green grass* we long

The patron saint is David,
The first of March his day,
When *Mae hen wlad fy nhadau,* the National Anthem
Is sung in that special way.

Coal was one of Wales' assets,
But now the mines have gone.
The pits were demolished some years ago,
But their valley communities live on.

Separated from England by two bridges now,
Yet we still must pay to come home,
But we don't mind, because when we arrive
It's on the *green, green grass* we roam.

Lucinda Highley

PROCLAIMING JESUS

Undaunted by the imminence of early morning mizzle,
A multitude of anoraks gave solace in the drizzle.
Huddled closely, collars raised, disregarding North Sea fret,
In Scarborough, stalwart Christians congregated in the wet.

Construction hammers flailed the air, securing the float's frame.
Steadfast, in pole position, a white banner bore His name.
Soggy song sheets quickly passed from hand to eager hand,
Encouraged by sweet music from the singers and the band.

The microphones connected. Songs soared to harmonise.
Salvation's exaltation, assaulted leaden skies.
Then joyfully, with Christian banners, vividly unfurled,
The *Global March for Jesus* awoke a holiday world.

Pauline Pullan

DERBYSHIRE NAMES

Derbyshire names, Derbyshire names.
Secret lives you conceal;
Listen while I list them now,
Their splendour to reveal.
Tissington and Hartington, and Alsop-en-le-Dale,
Where the old-time railway is now a walkers' trail.
Dalbury and Trusley, and Sutton-on-the Hill,
Lost among the country lanes, but living places still.
Miller's Dale, and Monsal Dale, and waters of the Wye
Softly singing Nature's hymns for every passer-by.
Long Lane and Bonsall Moor, where the Romans came,
Seeking for land and lead and imperialistic fame,
Cresswell and Whitwell and Crich Stand on the hill
Where those who cruelly died are remembered still.
Froggatt Edge and Stanedge, Millstone Edge too -
Rock-climbers' paradise, and with paradisal view.
From Bleaklow and Kinder among pathless peaty wastes
Down flows the Derwent; through Chatsworth Park it hastes
To the old mills of Belper, down the valley to the Trent,
Its energy for Derbyshire now completely spent.
More names for all of us will bring more memories back;
but better still, get up and out, with map and purse and pack,
and travel round the county with its names that sing the songs
of history, of passion, of ancient rights and wrongs.

P Wolstenholme

GOD'S OWN GARDEN

When I consider God's wonderful land,
the place He would most prefer,
is the garden planted by His hand,
The county of Denbighshire?

Denbigh is a market town,
overlooked by the castle keep,
from its high tower looking down,
the townsfolk look like sheep.

Saint Asaph is a busy place,
its Cathedral is so small,
But its people are full of grace,
God loves them one and all.

The county sweeps down to the sea,
It's seen from every hill,
From the Clwyd to the Dee,
from Prestatyn down to Rhyl.

Rhuddlan Castle stands strong and proud
Its profile never varies,
Here Llewellyn, our prince was crowned,
Overlooking the church of Saint Mary's.

Mountains, rivers, hills and vales,
God's own garden, our desire,
God's kingdom built here in Wales,
God's garden . . . Denbighshire.

Bill Hayles

LEEDS - CITY OF CONTRAST

Prince Edward sits, motionless, upon his blackened steed,
Standing guard, while traffic hurtles round and round,
And shire horses, gleaming, white and proud
Strut their stuff along the streets.

The Town Hall lions gaze, uncomprehendingly at the reclining figure
by Henry Moore, nextdoor.
Lunch-breaking business folk march smartly into up-market city stores,
Bypassing buskers in the nearby alleys,
Tootling tunes for two-pences.

The derelict mills, smart apartments, and Royal Armouries line the
            grimy river,
Home to kingfisher, swan and cycling students.
The river runs past rows of brick back-to-back homes, estates of
            executive housing
And solitary stone cottages, through leafy valleys and delightful dales,
From its birth-place beneath the rocky crags, to give Leeds life.

Helen Milton

GOING HOME

Shadows slowly forming on this final day
Angels they are singing to guide you on your way
Heavenly gates are opening to welcome you at last
And all life's weary trials are gone into the past
I feel your spirit with me each and every day
and know you're always with me as I walk along the way
Although my days are lonely and the nights are always long
I feel your warmth around me even though I know you're gone
But I must count my blessings, we loved each other to the end
And will always be so grateful for a husband and a friend
And when the day of judgement comes I know that we will be
Together in each other's arms for all eternity.

Marion James

WALES

Sometimes I breathe my dragon's fire
I sing my valley song
this rugged land a part of me
in truth where I belong

I can't forget where I was born
the sea runs in my veins
if my land fell tomorrow
I'd build from its remains

The land may not be vast and wide
so many say so small
its heart is of a giant
its pride and strength is all

When it spreads its golden rug
of our national flower
you cannot help but be part of
a sweet mysterious power

Then when it takes and haunts you
you must return once more
you'll find it's somehow in your blood
if you didn't know before

My dragon lives a freedom
no shiny knight can kill
he'll fly above, without clipped wings
each mountain and each hill

Hazel Houldey

THIS SACRED PLACE

Here great kings fought in battle, they died on this sacred ground
Isolated in this savage landscape,
Death cries slowly losing its soul, here at this sacred place born of
a sacred country.

Stand upon the rock and fill your eyes with wonder and beauty, snow
that's melted snow from the mountains now turned into crystal clear
water, mist that now swirls and rises to cloak the waterfall, rivers now
have carved its way through valleys and meadows there to leave its
mark, voices to be heard as whispers that are gently carried upon the
wind from centuries past.

This sacred place, this sacred country, home of kings and princes,
warriors, magicians stand at court lost in dreams, the fire in the great
hall casting shadows, flames from torches burning low, these great men
of wisdom now wait in silence for their fortelling.

The landscape changes from the deepest green to the wild rugged
seascape that leads to the outside world, sea of blue green, sea of black
when troubled or tormented, castles built of stone and life's blood stand
guard against the invader, songs of men tell of victory that are carried to
distant lands, the sound of the harp faint but pure and free of sin.

Old men tell stories around the campfire, in time boys become men and
tell the same stories of the battles won and lost, stories passed on to
each new generation in turn, secret words spoken of the same magic, as
one nation, its voice is turned into song, this will be heard as a strange
tongue throughout the world, the heart of the dragon beats strongly,
which gives life to this sacred place . . . to this sacred land.

Jeff Chick

A Welsh Octogenarian Remembers

In *The Good Old Days* we knew our fated place
In the God-forsaken, odd, mistaken scheme of things.
Born old, we wore our bodies sack-like, without grace,
Immune to light and laughter, soothing touch and stings.
School albums show us boxed in classroomed stocks,
That fettered brain and will as much as limb,
In adults' cut-down twill or shapeless smocks,
Like sepia shrouds; funereal and grim.
At play, we cloned screen heroes, tyrants, crooks;
Stampeded sheep and rodeo-rode a few;
Swarmed over hills; swung trees; swam silted brooks.
In dread of edging forward in life's queue,
Our terraced minds sought ledges: jobs that tore
Our hopes and dreams to shreds, then darned them whole
With promises of *Better, Different, More,*
To numb ambition and sedate the soul.
Men slaved in mines and docks; farmed hollow hills;
At awkward ease drank beer; blew brass; sang songs,
While women drudged and trudged to settle bills,
Too worn to wail the source of all their wrongs.
Each Sunday shrieking deacons drove us flock
To pens of varnished pews, where, pilchard-packed,
We gaped and gasped as preachers thrilled to shock
Us silly out of all the *sins* we lacked.
Yet, I remember best rare signs from heaven:
When banners beckoned home our war-worn youth,
And rostra rumbled with the roar of Bevan
Deafening false prophets with the din of truth.

Beryl Roberts

Days Gone By

'Tell me a story, Grandma
Of when you were young like me.
What did you do, where did you go?
Were there lots of things to see?'
I sat awhile, as my thoughts returned,
To the place that I called home
'When I was young' I then replied,
'We all lived on a farm, it nestled in a hollow,
With a river and a barn.
We'd cows and sheep and chickens,
There was always lots to do,
I'd be up in the morning, get washed in the yard,
Cold water woke me with a start, and then there'd be milk,
Straight from the cow, as father milked the herd.
Then off to school, with slate and chalk,
The best time was the autumn.
We'd gather conkers as we walked
And stuffed them in our satchels.
As the bell gave its final gong,
We shivering, shuffled in, but in the classroom,
Soon were warm, as we stood round the fire,
We sang our prayers, and tables too
In English and in Welsh, and sat entranced
As in story form, Welsh history did inspire.
As dusk fell, we ambled home, as lamp light
Lit each window, and neighbours called a greeting out,
Sometimes, a message for our mother.
So, my child, now you know what my young days were like,
Full of simple happiness of Welshness mixed with strife.'

Hillary Wickers

HE WILL ALWAYS RETURN

All his life he travelled
Countries far and wide
But of all the beauty he beheld
Something deep inside
Always drew him back to the
Yorkshire that he loved

Running streams, childhood dreams
Anchor at his heart
Although a travelling man
Not long could they both part

Back to Yorkshire's rolling hills
Oaks and Sunday roast
The things he always thought about
The things he loved the most

Will he wander yet again
Yes! Of course he will
But always he'll return
To Yorkshire's rolling hill.

Veronica X

GOOD LUCK TO THE WHITE ROSES OF YORK

So to Oldham you go in the merry month of May,
We all wish you a most successful day,
Hoping some trophy or cup you may win,
Once again to Northfield School honour bring.

Hoping the team's concentration doesn't flag,
or all your energy start to sag,
Find that the festival is first-rate,
Also the team achieve their best to date.

I know you all have worked very hard,
and your reputation you will have to guard,
If you all do your best that is the main,
For the festival you have really had to train.

Pamela J Earl

WELSH MOUNTAINS

Rambling and rugged mountains
Sides touched with streaks of grey,
Mist enshrouded summits
Ghosts some people say.

Standing guard forever patient
Forming our valleys and vales,
Steadfast, strong and undaunted
The very spirit of Wales.

In the depth of winter
They are topped with caps of white,
Shining steel helmets
Warriors waiting to fight.

These mountains have given protection
To our heroes of days gone by,
Given them the spirit to carry on
Not lie down and die.

Alas the mountains now stand alone
For our heroes have passed away,
But our spirit is forever strong
Waiting for the day.

Dennis William Roberts

THE JEWEL OF ALL CROWNS

Wales is like a precious stone,
Set in a crown of glorious landscape
Which rolls like hills into scenery
So beautiful, it steals the eye.
Mountains laze in tranquil moments
As daffodils line their feet like soldiers;
A fanfare of petals floats from golden trumpets
All rejoicing at spring's return.

Snowdonia, the Beacons cast a noble eye
Over this land of choirs and song;
Harmonies weave through spring's blossoming trees
Which now have leaves that are young.
Rivers of glass, meadows of green,
Silent sheep scattered like sculptured stones;
Industrial scars have now been healed
As fresh air now fills the once valleys of coal.

Wales is the land of my fathers,
A land built with strength and pride;
Chapel doors once wide open with welcome
Now shut like death's cold eyes.
This land's beauty has been captured
And set in a crown of its own,
This jewel defies fine words of description,
Not even a king's ransom for my home.

Gerald Thomas Wall

A TASTE OF WALES

Cardiff Castle, Oakwood Park,
Dan-yr-Ogof Caves where it is dark.
Caldey Island, Folly Farm,
All add to Wales' natural charm.

Pleasure beaches, historical towns,
Preseli Hills with its ups and downs.
Coastline walks and wildlife places,
Breathtaking views and friendly faces.

Caerphilly cheese and prime Welsh lamb,
Home-made cawl with leeks and ham.
Bara Brith and fresh Welsh cakes,
A warmer welcome no other place makes.

Helen Seal

SO GLAD I'M WELSH

Wales is a country quite small and yet strong,
A country renowned for Eisteddfod and song,
A country quite prosperous in business as well,
And is doing some good so the people can tell.
Its a beautiful country with mountains so steep,
Which are covered in heather and bracken and sheep,
The views are breathtaking from each lonely peak,
With Welsh as the language you'll hear people speak.
'Bore Da' is good morning, 'P'nawn Da' is good day,
They are happy and friendly in every way.
We love our rugby which we play from the soul,
You can hear shouts in England, when we've scored a goal,
There's a river between us, the Severn long and wide,
But I'm so very happy that I was born on this side!

Jane Thomas

THAT BEAUTIFUL SHORE

I left behind grim Merthyr Vale,
And drab Cefn Coed Y Cymmer,
And all at once I breathed the air,
And knew a Brecon summer,

I ceded Edward's castle grey
To Gwynedd's son and daughter,
And sighed a sigh for Glyder Fawr,
And knelt at Ogwen Water,

I went to Ystradfellte fair,
And walked behind a fountain,
As men went down for Tower coal,
I climbed the Rhigos mountain,

I shunned the bookish barren coast,
I took to Cambrian ridges,
And watched the Rheidol tumble down
Below demonic bridges,

I saw the falcon dip and dive,
The Tintern redwood quiver,
And marvelled at an abbey where
The sea becomes a river,

And now I leave grim Merthyr Vale,
And drab Cefn Coed Y Cymmer,
To seek a beauty far beyond,
To seek eternal summer.

Peter Davies

ONLY A YORKSHIRE LAD

Born In Yorkshire, in a village near a mine
There is plenty of dust, grit and grime
Lots of slag heaps, like mountains they seem
When covered in snow, the sun makes them gleam

Times were not easy, mostly hard
People grew veg in their little back yard
Miners kept greyhounds and pigeons to race
Trophies they won took pride of place

In the school holidays, I went picking peas
This was hard work, everyone agrees
The money they paid was two bob a sack
All the bending near broke your back

Most people are friendly, helpful and kind
Wherever you go, none better will you find
These times are much better, I'm ever so glad
And happy to be born a Yorkshire lad.

Ken Skinner

HUMBER BRIDGE

I have seen the bridge in many moods:
Brooding, when the mists of autumn shroud its towers;
Joyful, exuding an almost ethereal charm,
On summer days when the sun is bright;
Peaceful, sleeping under a blanket of stars
On a cold-clear, frosty winter night;
Shivering, as though afraid.
When lashed by springtime's gales and rains.
I have seen the bridge in many moods.
And marvelled at its graceful strength in all.

Richard Young

OUR YORKSHIRE

A visit to our Yorkshire,
This did we suggest one day.
The southerners responded,
Said with emphasis 'No way.'
They'd heard tales of our Yorkshire
Of some dark and smoky mills
And landscapes full of slag heaps,
Seen from grey and dreary hills.
A visit to our Yorkshire,
Once much later they did make.
This has not been intended,
It was really a mistake,
Had wished to see Leeds Castle,
For the Kent Leeds should have booked.
Hotel was in Leeds city,
One fact they had overlooked.
They found, in our Broad Acres,
Roundhay Park with much delight
And many real surprises
Were to come into their sight.
Leeds city was the gateway,
To the lovely Yorkshire dales,
With the space and matchless beauty,
In the glorious nature trails.
In Yorkshire now residing,
Ilkla Moor baht at their song
To us they are confiding,
'To our Yorkshire we belong.'

D J Price

SCARBOROUGH

Despite being, at times,
Decidedly cool
It overlooks the ocean
Like a precious jewel
With its refreshing sparkle
So truly appealing
To radiate such a warm
Welcoming feeling.

From high on the cliff tops
There's a wonderful view
The scene is invigorating
Magnificent too
As one surveys
The panorama below
Watching the rolling waves
Ebb and flow.

It is a Shangri-La
A wonderland
Complete with friendly folk
Sea and sand
So raise your glass
And drink a toast
. . . to Scarborough!
The pride of the Yorkshire coast.

B Hilditch

YORKSHIRE MY YORKSHIRE

Yorkshire my Yorkshire
When I think of thee
I remember the green fields
The streams running free.
And as a child
Would I ceaselessly roam
Past hedgerows and woodlands,
And dank mossy stones.
Now the harsh light of day
Sees my Yorkshire disturbed
The greed and deception
Leaves me perturbed,
Industrial estates
Fed by grim motorways
The wildlife endangered
Has seen better days.
Thus my anger boils over
As the fields disappear
I am losing my Yorkshire
Year by year.

Geoffrey Price

HALF-TERM BUS TO BAKEWELL

It was on a Monday morning,
On the Bakewell bus,
There were mums and dads and children,
Lasses and lads and - us.

'Just look at yon lad's purple hair,'
My auntie shouted out.
'Must be one of those punk rockers,
I've heard so much about.'

It was a happy journey,
We heard many a joke and chaff,
And it was one of the *punk rockers*,
Who caused the biggest laugh.

When he saw the sheep,
With the blue *herd mark*,
He yelled to his pal, Dunc,
'Hey, Kid, what do you reckon?
Even the sheep's gone punk!'

Sheila Markham

SONG OF YORKSHIRE

The broad acres of Yorkshire are homeland to me
From the slope of the Pennines and east to the sea
From the White Horse at Kilburn to the brave Ivanhoe

We sing about Yorkshire wherever we go.

The moors and its mountains, its rivers and dales
It's only a county much finer than Wales
The Danes came to Yorvick and stayed, don't you know

They sang about Yorkshire in the long, long ago.

The cricket at Scarborough, not to mention the fair
Bridlington Harbour and the Regatta, that's there
The Burning of Bartle, the Great Yorkshire Show

We sing about Yorkshire wherever we go.

The Lime Cove at Malham, the Black Dyke brass band
The Ribblehead viaduct that straddles our land
The bridge o'er the Humber that sways to and fro

We sing about Yorkshire wherever we go.

J Ellison

THRIDINGS

Down in the valley
Midst summer's dream
Lies a city so huge,
Where dwells England's cream

In the centre of Yorkshire
Of Britain, the world,
Where the greatest of knowledge
And talents unfurl,

Where the hardest of workers
And players of sport
Take pride in their labours,
And the dangers they court.

This wide city of Leeds
Creates Gentlemen scholars,
Pours forth graceful women,
And in family life wallows.

Their great talents do stretch
Up hill and down dale,
Throughout all of the Ridings
Its people prevail.

Lest any of them wander
And move far away
They'll always return
And come back to say,

'I've travelled afar
And met many new kinds,
But none are so carefree
Nor middling of mind

Than wise Yorkshire folk
The salt of the earth,
Born, in God's own county,
Inspired at birth.'

C Jones

NATURAL WONDERS

There are many wondrous things on earth
And all great sights to see,
But the splendour of the North York Moors,
Are a magic land to me.

In good weather the scene's majestic,
When bad, fills one with fear,
So compelled - I always will return,
To these sights that I hold dear.

The sheep are free to stray here,
Little lambs free from all danger,
Big men have found a deep content,
Never feeling like a stranger

It really is a wonder,
That on-one can deny,
This great expanse of beauty,
Where the heather hills meet sky.

Mere man alone could not construct,
The feel of nature and its wealth,
Because it's that little piece of Yorkshire,
That *God* keeps for himself.

Sue Geldard

MAGIC MOMENTS IN FILEY

Brass bands, barley sugar, hoops and hopscotch in the streets,
Clowns with painted faces - lots of fun!
Fine Edwardian ladies, Punch and Judy, juggling feats!
    Festive summer days for everyone.

Circling the crackling bonfire, jolly crowds ward off the heat,
Hot dogs, toffee-apples, colours bright.
Swooshing showers of stars and crackers, lots of friends to meet -
    Swish home through autumn leaves with pumpkin-light.

Well wrapped against the winter wind stride out along the beach,
The roar of waves and suddenly, sharp snow!
So hurry back to Christmas cheer and warmth of rosy cheeks -
    There's a Filey welcome all the year, you know!

    The turf feels soft. A cormorant flies across our lovely bay,
    While sparkling wavelets wash the morning shore.
    A skylark, warbling, rises through the heavenly blue day -
    Spring is arriving - who could ask for more?

L Mary Harrison

UNTITLED

Withernsea - my bus is here - I hope it's not too full -
I'm tired out, though pleasantly, while stopping here in Hull -
I've had the greatest fish and chips, a beer to wash it down
But - thankfully - my bus is here, and I can leave the town -

I'm going home, to Withernsea - a place I've grown to love
The heavy seas, the seagulls - all soaring up above
I love it all, so fresh, so clean, a map, a fishing rod -
Calmly wait to catch a fish - haddock or a cod -

The seniors at lunch time, are going into town
For fish and chips -a butty - the fish all golden brown -
It's good to see these young folk growing up so free -
Enjoying life and laughter in good old Withernsea

And even when they're older, and most will surely roam
They never, ever will forget - Withernsea - their home.
I can't say really what it its , that makes me love these parts
Except the Yorkshire people, and their lovely, great big hearts.

P M Whittaker

THE HUMBER BRIDGE

Have you driven 'cross the Humber Bridge,
on a hot and blistering day?
Cursing the traffic that is standing still, and
waiting in the queue to pay?
Have you stood atop the Humber Bridge,
when all the tide has left behind,
is a sea of oozing yellow mud that
seems to settle on your mind?

Then take some time to travel back
at a time when the sun is low
when the Humber burns with the golden fire
from a Yorkshire sunset glow.
Let Hessle foreshore beckon you,
on a walk you'll never forget.
'Neath an orange sky, the Humber Bridge
is a magnificent silhouette.

I am still discovering this different life,
and finding pleasures at each turn.
Now each time I cross the Humber Bridge,
I'm proud that Yorkshire is now my home.

Eileen Bailey

SCARBOROUGH CASTLE

Above a gull-bespattered cliff you stand,
battered and bruised.
As if the fierce grey waters
churning at your feet,
had grasped with icy fingers,
to fashion and re-fashion what other hands
had once begun.
No swarthy Romans tread your halls today.
No sentries search, with eagle eye,
for bright-sailed dragon ships
cleaving the wind-whipped waters of the bay.
Gaunt and beautiful, with head held high,
your tattered ruins brave the summer sun
and winter cold.
Haunted by wraiths of men long-gone,
your sole companions screaming gull,
you still remain
a stalwart guardian of our Yorkshire wold.

Jess Chambers

RIEVAULX DAWN

From the temple steps, the valley steeply dropped away,
'neath the terrace, high above, the ruined abbey lay.
Sunlight spilling through its arches, casting shadows long,
all about in summer fields came forth the dawn bird's song.

In times past the hillsides rang with bells which chimed below,
monks walked through the stately grounds, their plants and
                                    seeds to sow.
Praying in the dark hours there, bowed low on bended knees,
silent in the chapel far beneath the terrace trees.

Gone the sound of singing now and lost the sounding bell,
silent and deserted and yet still, all things are well.
Towering in the sunlight on this quiet summer morn,
stately Rievaulx still endures, once more to greet the dawn.

Richard Langford

A COUNTY'S LINK

Down mountain paths
          Through woodland dells
Coastlines with winding bays
          From highland tors and rolling fells
Along Britain's many byways.

Devon, to the coast of Cornwall
          From Scotland down to Wales
River and streamlets meander
          To mirror a picture
Of Yorkshire's wolds and dales.

In havens unfrequented
          By seaside and sandy bays,
Countryside, with historic sites
          Archaeological surveys
To portal Yorkshire's place in history
          It's heritage and ways.

The strongest link in a country chain
          Uniting north to southern hemisphere
From east and west to Lancashire
          The largest county in the land
Is Yorkshire's claim.

S V Smy

RIDING'S END

Not merely another county
More old-fashioned, independent State
With its own foreign language
and culture out of date.

Moorland hills to be proud of
Run-down cities to try and hide
Only those born and bred here
will ever get inside.

Heart of industrial England
The mines have taken their toll
Scarring innocent valleys
Hoping for sulphur-free coal

The best place to be if you live here
The last place on earth if you don't
Those who can are leaving
The flat caps and pigeons won't

Gone are the days of greatness
The Goliath of England no more
Destroyed by too many Davids
The south has evened the score

Mark Rooney

YORKSHIRE SENSE

The sounds, the tastes and smells of Yorkshire,
He'd forgotten all these years.
A shock they were to his fine senses,
Senses that had ceased to hear.

To hear the cry of curlews calling,
High above the silent fells.
Stirred his heart until it leapt up,
Leapt up as it seemed to fill.

Seemed to fill each dormant taste bud,
Until they woke up once again.
To tastes that only could be Yorkshire's
Like Yorkshire's puds and Yorkshire's ales

He smelt the hills and dales around him,
As bracing Yorkshire breezes stirred,
A sense that's now forever wakened,
Wakened to his Yorkshire birth.

Tess Thomas

RAINCLIFF

On Raincliff Hill mid thorn and whin
I hear the thrush and blackbird sing
and stroll beneath the leafy trees
listening to the rustling leaves.

Loudly on a summer day
comes the song of the noisy jay.
The mallard and the coot I hear
calling from the quiet mere.

In Raincliff Woods where tall trees grow,
in bright sunshine's filtered glow,
I wander far from noisy throng
and hear a robin chirp his song.

When fleecy clouds glide o'er the sky
a greenfinch calls his notes on high.
A woodpecker hammers out his lay
and noisy starlings greet the day.

When evening shadows softly fall
I hear the sweetest song of all.
A nightingale declares his love
and trills his song to God above.

John S Bertram

Away Days

Gold-leaf sky . . .
patterned with flocking
bird heading for
roosting trees in
squirrel wood
. . . covers me
as I sleep on
peacock-feathered lawn
circled by fairy
rings weaving magic
through my dream
where restless swallows
carry me
over russet moorland peaks
to some faraway
homeland

Barbara Allen

The Ouse

Wide, winding, watery river, grey and green
Flowing majestically through York
Overhung with attractive bridges
Lendal, Ouse and Skeldergate
River laden with boats, boats and tripper boats
These to Bishopthorpe Palace and back
Or to Naburn Lock and on
Passing lush, verdant fields on either side
Sun shining, blue sky
Is this not the epitome of bliss?

Anne Powell

In Praise Of Filey

I walked on the beach at Filey
With the wind blowing through my hair,
The sand was wet beneath my feet,
My mind was free of care!
Children were playing happily,
Building castles in the sand,
The sea was like a lover's kiss,
Paying court onto the land.

But even as those children played
An emergency call was being made.
A gale blew up beyond the bay,
As nature tossed her seas that day.
One fishing boat far out at sea,
Had suffered a catastrophe
The lifeboat crew, responded fast,
And put to sea, the die was cast.

For hours they fought that raging storm,
To save those men in need,
Our lifeboat crew in finest form
Were Filey men indeed!
Though battered by gigantic waves
They struggled on, those Filey braves,
So this is why, for all my days,
You'll find me singing Filey's praise.

J S Rowley

YORKSHIRE'S BEST

How fortunate we are, we Yorkshire folk
To be blessed with the moors and the dales,
How lucky we are, able to ramble
Through pleasant green valleys and vales.

The scenery is magnificent, breathtaking,
As the sun rises up over the dale
On the light wind that gently rustles the trees
Is carried the call of pheasant and quail.

The whinnying of horse, the bleat of sheep and lamb
Bid us good morning as we pass them by,
The willows on the riverbank sway in the wind,
No weeping willows these, but the wind seems to make them sigh.

The river flows on so majestically,
He babbles, sparkles and sings,
Anglers sit patiently by his side
All hoping for bigger things.

The river flows on by the old water mill,
A mill long forgotten, derelict beyond repair,
Old water wheel has not turned for many a long day,
The mill's work now is done elsewhere.

Birds wheel in the sky at sunset,
A perfect day draws to a close in the dales,
The warm, friendly atmosphere of the local inn beckons
With its promise of fine Yorkshire ales.

Yorkshire in all its natural beauty,
What more can a man ask than that,
Unless it's to hear a brass band play
'On Ilkley Moor baht 'at.'

Frederick Sowden

YORKSHIRE

Yorkshire, once famous for dark satanic mills
Together with its large factories and smoking chimneys
Presented a scene of murky gloom to any stranger
Here in my Yorkshire

Today the scene is changed with new buildings
That bustle with high finance, commerce and tourism
Whilst conservationists try to preserve the best of yesterday
Here in my Yorkshire.

Think also of dark hills highlighted by winter's snow
Where sunlight and shadows dapple each dale
And hidden villages with picturesque dry stone walls are also
Here in my Yorkshire.

Brass bands that play with true Northern spirit
And choral societies singing Messiah to you
For music is an important part of our lives
Here in my Yorkshire.

This county, once famous for its cricket
Is a place where sportsmen are still spoken of in hallowed tones,
For we never forget those who served us well
Here in my Yorkshire

There are also many great inventions
For example, a certain pudding springs to mind
Served with roast beef, it's a dish for you to savour
Here in my Yorkshire

The wide variety in this greatest of counties
Is matched only by the uniqueness of her people
Who remain fiercely independent, honest, reliable and true
Here in my Yorkshire.

Mavis Simpson

A LITTLE YORKSHIRE RELISH

'I can tell you come from Yorkshire'
I've heard that said more than once
Something to do with the way we speak
Wholesome as a ploughman's lunch
We may seem to be hard-headed
And yes, we call a spade a spade
But we'd fight to the death for what we believe
Willing hands helping those ill and afraid,
Silent now, giant mills who
Spun wool for all the world.
The grass grows green on abandoned mines,
Where once Britain's coal was hurled
But time moves on, we're still the best
At whatever we turned our hands to
Like Yorkshire beer and Yorkshire puddings
Roast beef for Sunday dinner
A little flutter on a horse
Though not everyone's a winner
'There's nowt as queer as folk' we say
And laugh with understanding
Cloth cap image, shawl and clogs,
Makes way for Haute couture
Leaders in culture old and new
Take Leeds, need I say more
Surrounding us, breathtaking beauty
Unchanged for a hundred years
Our Yorkshire dales and purple moors
Help forget life's trials and fears.
So if you're listening, God, we thank you
For these great gifts of yours.

W E McTeigue

WHITBY

Town of lost ships.
Early morning seagulls cry you awake.
Down the Khyber Pass, through the short-cut snicket,
To the harbour teeming with jostling fishing boats,
Whose Scottish brothers had wakened from their winter sleep,
To find spring had arrived
Bringing the miracle of re-appearing herring.

Those days of my youth we would jump
From one boat to another
And on the solid phalanx of the Lower Harbour
Walk over the water, claiming no supernatural powers.
The masts were a forest of movement.
Strong winds would roll the waves over the harbour claws.
The boats would tug fiercely at their moorings,
Their rigging tattoo dinning your ears.

Raise your eyes to see gentle Hilda
Midst the ruined stones of her graceful abbey
Keeping watch over the nestling, squat church below,
Whose pews were made from the timber of wrecked boats.

But turn to the beaches where winds' hidden fingers
Will throw sand into your eyes.
Contours of the dunes will re-shape despite clutching marram.
Sea birds taxi down, throwing up their feet.
They brake to a halt to peck at chosen pickings.
Search diligently at the foot of fallen cliffs.
One of Hilda's snakes, an ammonite, may be exposed,
Or the skull of a seagull, or a piece of Whitby jet.
But don't linger too long.
Your coffee will be waiting at Botham's.

Raymond Bradbury

SWALEDALE

This rugged dale with valleys green
Scenic views so rarely seen
Moors rich with purple heather
Kind folk who like to stop and blether

Old stone houses in hamlets sparse
Sheltered from weather, known to be harsh
The calling of curlews and grouse on the moors
Gives pleasure untold to many viewers.

Leisurely fishermen on the fast flowing Swale
Calm and peaceful, this heavenly dale
So tranquil yet active, as tradition moves on
When farming passes from father to son

Deep ravines on Buttertubs Pass
Sheep on hillsides searching for grass
Among the crags so steep they roam
In this rugged dale - nature's own

The lead mines and smelt mills of long, long ago
Reveal hardship endured with courage, we know
Their ruins are reminders of life past in this dale
As we listen and learn from many a tale.

Doris Thorpe

YORKSHIRE MOORS

A place of dreams, of reflection, of peace
A time where life's heavy pace may cease
To feel the wind and hear your own soul
A place to be able to reach your goal.

A world of colour, of texture, of sound
A place to feel the earth under the ground
To feel above all of that below
A place to feel the sun's pure glow

A world of mist, of rains, of snow
A place where life continues to grow
To feel the past and what could be
A place to go as far as you can see

A Yorkshire of dreams, of history and past
Magnificent in beauty to the last
Always the haven, to seek, to rest
This is England at its very best.

Hazel Graham

WHITBY HARBOUR

From high above the sandy shore
we watch the waves and hear their roar,
beside me in this special place
I gaze upon your windswept face.

The cliffs are where you long to be
to look down on the rolling sea,
to point at seagulls as they glide
above the early morning tide.

Along the winding paths we walk
as nature's marvels fill our talk,
the sun breaks through the cloudy sky
and brings a sparkle to your eye.

The Abbey fades as we descend
the steps that never seem to end,
your smile suggests a shopping spree
along the cobbled streets we see.

Through summer days and winter nights
we like to visit these quaint sights,
for it is always fun to be
at Whitby Harbour by the sea.

Charlie McInally

THANKFUL INDEED

What links the inland village of Cundall
And its neighbour Norton-le-Clay,
To the seaside village of Cayton
Nestling peacefully by the bay?

The link, for which they're so grateful,
Is that there is no need to be seen
A World War One memorial
To the dead on each village green.

Hence each is termed a 'thankful' village
Of which Yorkshire can boast but four,
Catwick being the other one
Ne'er to have sadness at a door.

Later years have seen wider conflict
And minor wars by the score,
Oh that the world could be at peace
With each home thankful evermore.

Norman Spence

MARKET WEIGHTON AND SURROUNDING

The beauty of unusual quietness
Through the hills to sky
And the breathless trees and walking winds
Where birds sit and fly

The burst of rain then sun again
Gives enormous pleasure too
Banqueting sights for eyes to see
Are here for me and you

O' come along and share with me
This place of green and brown
For this is my home of splendour mass
Overlooking my wonderful town.

Richard H Cary

YORKSHIRE PRIDE

From White-Horse hills to Scarboro's coast
There's no finer scenes than ours, we boast,
Who wants to go across the sea
When all you need is in Whitby.

Or roam upon the glorious dales
Follow round those nature trails,
Meander through the quaintest scene
Robin Hood's Bay is where I mean.

Or should you enter the town of York
Tread upon the bar-wall walk,
See the Minster in its glory
Go inside and hear its story.

And who can say they've not been there
In ancient abbeys to stand and stare,
Where ruined cloisters once stood strong
In mind you hear the monks in song.

Whether by land or by the shore
With all its scenes that I adore,
It is so very plain to see
Yorkshire is the place for me.

Agnes Cook

HULL IS WHERE THE HEART IS

The Gaul is now but a ghost
Snatched away in a mist
Still shadowy figures wait for loved ones
to return from their shift.

The fishing trade which once thrived
Has also vanished, along with the men
But still some veterans of that bygone era,
by telling their stories,
keep the gap between past and present nearer.

Each line in their face illustrating both passion and pain
Hoping their memories won't be washed away in the rain.

'Hull is where the heart is.' That's what old Evelyn says
As she sips tea from her mug and ponders on her phrase
'I've had a good life, all said and done.
But I do wonder where the Gaul has gone.'

Karen Jarvis

MY YORKSHIRE HOME - WITH LOVE

To stand and watch the rivers flow,
Not ever knowing where they go,
The old stone walls built by muscle and sweat,
The toil of man we shall never forget,
The winding roads lead to farms in the distance,
No one can disturb their lonely existence,
The homes are safe surrounded by dale,
Centre of village - the pub - with its ale,
Churches, with history, famous people now gone,
Memories for visitors will always live on,
All 'round the country each has its own,
But Yorkshire for me is where I call 'home'.

W Render

BIRTHPLACE HAUNTS OF YORK'S FAWKES

In York's alleys and courts does Guy Fawkes stalk?
His ghost but a shadow, perhaps a mere wisp,
In 'Coffee Yard' or his birthplace 'Petergate'?
Is his spirit in that cobbled nook
Or in an oak-beamed inn by 'Stonegate'?

Hauntingly a low chuckle from a dark doorway
May send a shudder through the unwary in 'Minster Gate'.
Somewhere in the fog of an ember night
And in the chill of a shivered November
Ghostly whispers warn wanderers to remember
To look and peer over one's shoulder!

Keep watch! Be bolder!
Trust not the touch paper in his now cold finger.
Better that you 'spark on' and do not linger
In those York alleys and courts where Guy Fawkes stalks.

R Peter Smith

WE HAVE IT ALL IN YORKSHIRE

We have countryside and beaches
We have hills and we have dales
We have beauty beside rivers
We have tranquil sunny vales
We have cities
We have villages
And market towns between
Cliffs that overhang the sea
And meadows grassy green
But amidst these Yorkshire riches
The greatest joy by far
Is the welcome we will show you
Because that's just how we are.

Hilda Slater

My Home Town Of Filey

I will always bless the day I was born, in England as green as can be
But even more because I was born in Filey by the sea,
Filey is a wonderful town, a gem on the eastern coast
But wherever people originate, they love their home town most
My home town's full of memories, they're what I love the best
High on the cliffs in the old churchyard, is where my loved ones rest.
The beautiful church of St Oswald stands, where I was baptised
                                                        and christened
But 'twas the Ebenezer Chapel, to my first bible stories I listened
On Union Street too stood the old infants' school, where at five
                                                    I spent my first days
Although it's long gone I can still see it yet, for deep in my
                                                    memory it stays
But my favourite was the senior school, that on West Road was set
The boy I eventually married, that was the first place we met,
And when I walk down Queen Street, it's the old Queen Street I see
Old Spring Row with fishermen's lines, outside cottages quaint
                                                        as can be,
In autumn we'd walk down church ravine, gathering logs brought
                                                    down in a storm
They helped eke the coal out in winter and keep the house
                                                    cosy and warm
And still when I feel lonely, or I've a problem I need to set free
My footsteps always lead me down, to the ever-changing sea.
To me the sea always gives comfort, it soothes all my troubles away
Especially when the moon is full making a pathway across Filey Bay
Standing alone on the cliff top or with bare feet in the sand on the shore
Gazing up at the starlight above me, I couldn't wish for anything more
You can keep all the bright lights and cities with all the rushing
                                                    and noise
I'll take the peace and quiet of Filey, it would be forever my choice
If there really is reincarnation, a hope in my heart there will burn
With my family and friends to this heavenly place of Filey
                                                    I'd wish to return.

Jean Rounding

UP NORTH

The Yorkshire of my childhood days
'Ridings' that I once knew
Kirkstall Abbey gardens
Where beautiful black tulips grew
Rivers, streams and countryside
Marred by pit hills and coal tips
Yet - Guiseley was the birthplace
Of Harry Ramsden's fish and chips!

Leeds Town Hall lions did walkabouts
At midnight? I was there!
The Black Prince sat astride his horse
In our famous City Square
I went boating on Roundhay Lake
Then the Mansion - buttered pikelets for treats
Back-to-back houses, chimney smoke
Wash-lines stretched across cobbled streets.

Knaresborough - evacuated there in '39
Petrified toys at Mother Shipton's cave and wishing well
Trips to Scarborough, Filey, Bridlington
And Whitby - a town with Dracula tales to tell
York, the Minster and city of ancient walls
Shook hands across the narrow street - The Shambles
Otley Chevin - uphill struggling cars
Ilkley Moor 'ba-tat' the place for rambles

Funny things I remember - men wore cloth caps for their pains
In icy January weather - car wheels wore skid chains
6d was a tanner, 10/- half a quid
'Eee by gum', them days were fun, when I was just a kid.

Freda Baxter

SUNDERLAND

Red and white are the colours
Football is the game and the
Stadium of Light is the latest
claim to fame.
A church by the river and a
saintly man named Bede give
cause for veneration among
the local breed.
Now stands St Peter's Campus
where shipbuilders once applied,
their skill in building proud ships
to sail the oceans wide.
Green and pleasant walkways
now pass where pit wheels stood
The black-faced work-worn miners
have surfaced now for good.
Towns of heavy industry are
seldom seen as pretty but
from the dust of days gone by
now rises this new city.

J M Collins

TYNE AND WEAR

Seaburn and Roker are lovely places,
Lots of sea and sand, and wide open spaces.
Whitburn and Shields not far away
Plenty to do on a summer's day.

Many hotels along the coast
Lovely food, they have a right to boast
A nice big fairground for the children to play
Take them in there and you've made their day.

For your holiday, this is the place to be
In a hotel along the coast of the North Sea
Watch from your window the miles of sand
Young lovers walking hand in hand
Fishermen fishing on Roker Pier
'Oh! This beautiful area of Tyne and Wear.

Patricia A M Lawson

VALLEY BRIDGE

Monotonous winter gusts
pierce bouquet-decked railings,
ignoring oriental missives
on overhead safety grids.

Penned in Chinese

Ravenous wind-licked
yellow ribbon bows,
hungry for attention
wave from the edge.

Tasteless memorials tease

Daily reminders of mortality
competing with the elements,
as penance for pedestrians
on route to work.

Are thought to appease

Further on, familiar forces
mock remnants of a man's tie,
in deference to the child
that fell with him.

Blessed release.

A Smith

A Stormy Night At Hornsea

The sea front stands in isolation -
Saturated by the rains
From Esplanade to Wilburs Market
Gurgling waters fill the drains.

At parish church against the tower -
Scaffolding drips wet and grey
Trees hang heavy damp with moisture.
The rains have never stopped all day.

At Hull Road corner puddles gather -
Stream dyke runs in spated flow
A canine skulks all wet and scraggy
Looking for a place to go.

Sand is thrown over the roadway -
As rising swells dash angrily,
Against the huge dark heavy boulders
Peeping out, above the sea.

At 'Promenade' the seagulls gather
Grabbing at discarded bread,
A feline stray - wet, cold and hungry,
Cowers in the old rose bed.

From Flamborough Head, the lighthouse
                              glimmers,
Throwing out her stems of light
Along the isolated coastline
Ravished by the stormy night.

Malcolm Wilson Bucknall

HARVEST FESTIVAL

A robin on a hawthorn branch
Lifts up his head to call.
Come, eat, you little creatures
Take from the harvest stall.

Jet beads of elderberries hang
And, catching the morning light,
Dewdrops shine like diamonds
No jewels are more bright.

Here are hips and haws and blackberries
And, down by the dry-stone wall,
Mushrooms gleam, half-hidden,
A plenteous feast for all.

A feast before snow starts to fall
As our caring Father planned,
The robin calls again to all,
'Come, eat from His bounteous hand.'

Out beyond the hedgerow
No vista is so grand,
The sun chasing cloud shadows
Across the rolling land.

Trees of gold and red and brown
And sparkle of the rills,
In distant blues and misty grey
Yorkshire's beloved hills.

Gill Gibbs

THE EMIGRANT

Scottish, Welsh and Yorkshire seed,
On England's soil, the garden grows
A shoot carved from Lakeland stone
His laughter sweet, this place he knows

But all is ripped, cast to sea
And with no charted course it steers
The sails full, the prow cuts clean
Down below, is a hold of fears

Years have passed, new earth is found
Little roots venture down once more
Into mountains and prairies
With skies so huge a dream can soar

The planes and phones try to keep
Contact with those we love the most
Dwell not on the loss of touch,
Smiling eyes or a Sunday roast

No voyage starts, no journey's end
Less a step is took, from the pier
Our hearts still pump the same blood
The same stars shine on us here.

Phill Read

HAVE YOU VISITED

Have you visited the city of Sunderland before
Come and see what we have in store
Streets full of people, that will make you smile
Not far from the sea, not even a mile.

Nissan cars are turned out galore
We were famous for making ships before
Our shops are busy, give them their due
Even if you have to stand in a queue.

You won't be alone, to stand by yourself
No one here gets left on the shelf.
If I left here I would shed a tear
Nowhere else would be so dear.

Dorothy McQuillan

SEABURN

From my window I can see the sea
It has a calming relaxing effect on me
Sometimes it's rough and very wild
Other times it's calm and mild
Every day come rain or shine
Just being there makes me smile
Seaburn is a wonderful place to live
If I sing its praises you must forgive
On Wednesday in my favourite spot
I even saw the royal yacht
In the conservatory at the bay
I wouldn't swap with Andrew even for a day.
A prince amongst men he may be
On the sea shore I am as good as he
I just love looking at the sea
Lots and lots of people speak to me.
If you travelled far and wide
A friendlier bunch you would not find
I'd never live anywhere I couldn't see the sea
So when I die please don't bury me
Just scatter my ashes on the seashore
I'll be happy at Seaburn for evermore.

Elsie Cooperwaite

THE NEW CITY

Take a boat from Roker two miles out to sea
Look back at the coastline and see what is to be,
Gone are all the shipyards and the cranes have too
The wheel of Wearmouth colliery completely gone from view.

St Peter's church surrounded by the University
The houses and the yachts in the marina by the sea.
Gone are the workmen Lowry portrayed with peak cloth caps,
The miners and fishermen, rat catchers with their traps.

We're looking, yes, at Sunderland, England's newest city
With all the new buildings is becoming rather pretty,
The bridges, the shopping centre attractively designed
The convenience of the shoppers, very much in mind.

Now we have the students with jeans and trendy gear,
Studying in Sunderland confident and without fear,
Students' accommodation multiplying and coming into view.
Very security-conscious for young people's safety too.

The local council's planning the future to arrange,
For the people of this city welcome the gradual change,
Looking forward, I am sure we are going to find
Sunderland University, a very special kind.

The golden sands of Roker and Seaburn Bay
The fairground, the Seaburn Centre, entertainment every day.
Yes, Sunderland's progressing into a tourist attraction,
Giving local people pride and satisfaction.

Christine Ridley Henderson

UNTITLED

When I was just a little lad
I wasn't good, but not too bad
And for to pass the time of day
My mates and I would want to play!

Now over Sunderland's River Wear
There is a bridge from there to here
Supported by an arch of steel
So high it made our senses reel!

The arch was formed with metal plates
Criss-crossed with steel struts interlaced
And at the sides a wire guard
In panels about one square yard.

One day we found that if you tried
To squeeze you could then climb inside,
A little gap was at the base
For adults difficult to trace,
Bridge experts like my mates and I
Could get in easily if we try!

So many times we went to play
Have fun and pass the time of day
For we would climb the bridge inside
And then slide down the other side.

On looking back we were such chumps
To slide across the rivet's bumps
On Sunderland's gigantic slide
Across the bridge at Wearside.

R E Nelson

GOLD OLD SUDDICK

Those were the days in good old Suddick
We went to bed we didn't lock doors.
No fitted carpets just clippy mats on the floors.
All the kids in Jowett Square took their bait
                  down Thompson Park
And it was safe for young and old in the dark.
No fighting or swearing everyone was so caring.
Mary Ann in the square, she sold hot pies and peas.
I would nip over on Fridays and buy some for our tea.
There was Little Joe shaking his pigeon corn tin
'Away lads,' he'd shout hoping to get one or two strags in.
My loving mother worked hard for her pay
Washing stacks of dirty dishes in a hotel called The Bay.
These are some of the things I remember with pride
I still live and breathe in good old Suddick
And it's something I would never want to hide.

Margaret Hunter

SUNDERLAND AFC

S tokeo's lads won the FA Cup in 1973,
U nited still they stand this day, in Reidy's company.
N ow in the year of '97, Roker Park did bite the dust,
D own in the archives now to be, a memory in trust.
E very single fan to date, remembers with fond regret
R ed army's true home, a place they'll never forget.
L egendary moments recorded and kept for posterity
A football team to top the rest, and go down in history.
N ow in the Stadium of Light, their home forever more
D eep in the hearts of fans today, is still the Roker Roar.

Joan Williamson

THE RIVER WEAR

I stand and watch in wonder,
The heron catching bait,
I stand and watch in wonder,
The minnows' darting gait.
I stand and watch in wonder,
The colours of the sky,
I stand and watch in wonder,
I stand and say goodbye.

I stand and hear in wonder,
The buzzing of the bees,
I stand and hear in wonder,
The whispering of the trees.
I stand and hear in wonder,
The dripping of the dell,
I stand and hear in wonder,
I stand and say farewell.

I stand and think in wonder,
How fast the river flows,
I stand and think in wonder,
Of where the water goes.
I stand and think in wonder,
Of the trees that grow so tall,
I stand and think in wonder,
Of the One that made us all.

Daniel Sullivan (11)

SUNDERLAND MY CITY

When I was young I dreamed
Of living in a country lane
Had passing thoughts of winter
In the sunny clime of Spain
On holidays I go each year
To countries hot and pretty
But as each break draw to a close
I long for my own city.
There are places that are finer
Of that there is no doubt
But Sunderland is home to me.
That's what it's all about
Memories of childhood
People that I know
Roots put down far in the past
A place that I've seen grow.
I worked and played in Sunderland
And grumbled like the rest
But never will I leave it
For to me it's still the best.

Ann Leonard

A421

Are those hills really gifts of nature,
Or are they formed from many tons
Of brick dust to the scene?

Are they waste, clumped and dumped,
Just, dust and earth combined,
Or are they pure,
Predominating spreads of green?

Old or young, I cannot know.
Do I admire fair replica,
Or is it true and pleasant land,
Which is forever England?

Irene Hayden

OUR NEW CITY OF SUNDERLAND

Our city stands proud and so bold
Its streets may not be paved with gold
but we are proud of our city as we grow old.

Sadly the shipyards and pits have all gone
but we will gladly struggle on.

On the Wearmouth pit site now stands
our new city football ground called
The Stadium of Light.

The Doxford Park is attracting jobs
from far and wide to our new city
with big firms like London Electricity.

On the other part of our city big car
giants like Nissan. Other firms don't
know what they're missing.

Our city library and museum is a must
for visitors to our city it seems.

Our 'shops and bridges shopping malls'
is a must for latest fashions.
It caters for all ages with all the leading
names, likes of C&A where everyone
                              meets their pals.

Edward Wray

BRIGHT LIGHTS OF WEARSIDE

When the working week is done,
Everyone wants to have some fun.
Forget their worries,
Party all night,
Live life to the full,
Head for Wearside's bright lights.
The pubs, clubs, the atmosphere,
Bright lights, friendly faces
and of course the beer.
The streets of Wearside come to life at night,
Crowds of people, an amazing sight,
New people meet,
Old friends unite,
To share laughter and fun,
every Friday night.
So for a special night out,
which you'll never forget,
the bright lights of Wearside are definitely best!

Louise Allison

GLASGOW

My aunt from Glasgow has a terrible habit
Of dancing while cleaning the drains,
Her left hand looks like a dragon
And her eyes open and shut like doors.
When we had tea and toast her great Dane
Knocked over the milk then dragged my coat down the lane.
My aunt said, 'It serves you right, you shouldn't
Have thrown a stone at Daisy the dog.'
I agreed I had done wrong, then I packed my case
And left the house to catch a train to Dundee,
In the fog.

Kenneth Mood

A SUNDERLAND CHILDHOOD

Remember a time, not long ago,
But then maybe it is,
When things were simple, streets were safe,
And all your friends were kids.

After the bath, with towel wrapped round,
Head on Mam's knee, the dickies were found,
Fine-tooth-comb wielded with practised hand,
And nits were sent to the promised land.

Watching in darkness the coal fire bright,
Casting its glow and warming the night.
Imagine pictures the embers would make,
Constantly changing as the coals would cake.
The hiss of the gas lamp above your head,
With a hot water bottle,
And a po under the bed.

Remember a time

Pocket money day and a trip to the shops,
Arrow bars, Spanish and rhubarb rocks.
Coconut macaroons, cinnamon sticks liquorice laces,
Smiling faces.

Then walk to the baths at the top of High Street
And afterwards another treat.
A penny dip from over the road,
The gravy burning your tongue,
The saveloy sticking in your teeth,
It was tremendous fun.

Gordon O'Leary

GREAT TIMES

Aeroplanes and motor cars ball bearings and pumps.
All these have helped Luton to come up trumps.
You visit an airshow watch a Provost fly by.
And just image all things pumps and bearings help drive
The tranquillity of Wardown Park with wood hitting wood
Boaters and shady hats protect from the sun.
Do not forget the beauty of the church with green surround
Nor to forget the college standing there
Giving of its best a future all can share
Display your plants, trees and flowers
How they brighten the town
Never forget all these things from which Luton has grown
Remember those old buildings sadly now gone
Let the future make Luton the one.

K M Wilson

A LITTLE VILLAGE NEAR SUNDERLAND

As a child I walked down through the cornfields to see
scarlet poppies winking at me
And among the golden corn so fair
I spied, sweet harvest mice playing there
Crossing over the Lonnin and into the meadow
I found buttercups and daisies scattered around
Red ladybirds I spied as I was passing by
who flew away in the wink of an eye
Going down the Gill steps to the riverside
I saw, garlic and bluebells growing far and wide
All this beauty and what did I hear?
The wind in the trees and birds calling near
Childhood meant freedom and ability to see
The wonder and beauty that God gave to me.

Anne Armstrong

A YEAR IN KILMUN

Folk ask. 'Are you fine, what d'you do with your time?'
I'm not sure, but I fill it in well.
There's the sea to be scanned, while the garden is planned,
And dreams dreamed that I scarcely can tell.

I have sailed o'er the Clyde, on a clear mill pond tide
When the hills were all covered in snow,
And a full sun beamed high, from an unadorned sky,
And my heart swell made humble tears flow.

There was treasure galore, cast adrift on the shore
After gales shed their cargo in force,
But when warm, on a whim, in the loch I did swim,
And folk thought it was Nessie off course.

The summer sun burned, and the landscape was turned
To a scene more resembling Crete,
With the evenings so fine, that outside we could dine,
With the midges full into retreat.

Then autumn delights, brought such wonderful sights,
As the rowans burst full into flame,
And the whole rich array, of nature's display,
Put humankind's triumphs to shame.

A robin now comes, and we share a few crumbs,
As he gives me the late forest news,
And I certainly find, that the turn of his mind
Is more fruitful than Cabinet views.

You must realise, I have found paradise,
And with one neat historic correction,
When we voted to gain, our Parliament again,
Came the year's final act of perfection.

Janette Valentine

SOMETHING BEAUTIFUL IS OUR LAND

The tips of gentle waves sway along
their movements sing graceful songs
Sparkling and shimmering, the sun
plays with the dawn
Building a new day to life's
Summer morn

Sereneness of the glorious skies
Growing in misty hue
The shade of warmness, glorious blue
A streak of white candy, the wisdom
of cloud
Take joy of the beauty,
shout it out loud

Fresh breath of life
something beautiful you bring
Blow away the strife
each moment nature bears her spring

Colours of this land aglow
rainbow's palette forever flow
Change the shaded glen
bring alive the emerald gem

And something beautiful lives on
from ocean's shore to gay hawthorn
Timeless wonder proud
pull away the invisible painter's
shroud

Loud we hear the rains
the glow of drops against
highland grains
The smell of freshness drives
our very souls
to something beautiful and
in our lives remains.

Frances James

You Are My River

There is a great river which flows to the sea
By Eastgate and Stanhope and green Hamsterley
   It meanders through Durham on the way to the shore
The old river Wear I love and adore.

   You brighten up Finchdale and Chester-le-Street
At Witton and Escomb you are a real treat
   Then you flow through to Weardale as strong as you can
To beautiful Frosterley and Wolsingham.

   My river has seen many nations and laws
Romans Vikings and the Danish have come to our shores
   You have seen every war in our long history
But the river I love still flows down to the sea.

   My river gives life to the mountains and fells
Then flows o'er the rocks through the forests and glens
   Your beauty and splendour I love and adore
And deep in my heart you will live evermore.

   For you are my river
Mother nature made your spirit free
   My beautiful river
Flowing down from the hills to the sea.

Robert Colvin

THE BEGINNING

This flaking hulk of a black oak canoe is believed to be our first
foray into the art of river navigation.
Unearthed at Hylton, it is the primitive ancestor
of the squat wooden ships built by Thomas Menvill,
the Wear's first official shipbuilder, to bolster the King's defences.

In his wake came the industrialists, studding the banks
with tiny yards, casting bluff barques and brigs
into the rising tide of the new world. Seemingly delicate
tea clippers ghosted the waters,
their precious cargo snug within its iron frame.

Later, cheering crowds lined the smog bound river bank
to bless the ponderous steel bodies sliding into the gully,
submerging those nearest waist deep in silted water,
a sign of luck. Acrid smoke hung as smaller traffic
skirted down toward the open water.

Under the bridge now all is quiet. Banked by new
developments the river eddies against the changing tide,
but if you close your eyes you may just hear an engine,
feel the presence of a towering vessel gliding past.

Angela Rose

JEWELLED SHORES

Her hills are clad in deepest amethyst
Her snow capped mountains by pale sun kissed
And emerald skirts her sapphire lochs.

Her glens, seen through ethereal mists,
Her history held secure as in a clenched fist.
Castles standing proud, her people prouder still.

Though many have settled far from here,
I'm sure they must often dream of Scotia's jewelled shores.

Marilyn Mcleod Wilson

ISLE OF SKYE

Oh Isle of Skye you've captured my heart
you've cast your spell on me
What secrets do your mountains hold
and your glens of mystery
What lurks behind your misty peaks
where birds of prey soar high
What are these tales being whispered
by winds that gently sigh
I hear those muffled echoes
amidst your jagged hills
I sense a mood of bygone days
that strangely calms and stills
To wander on your hillsides
to tread upon your sand
Gives a feeling of contentment
on this beautiful island
Your rivers, lochs and seaways
are etched upon my mind
It's sad when I must leave
all this peacefulness behind
Oh Isle of Skye you've welcomed me
you've made me feel a part
And one day I'll return to you
for it's where I've left my heart.

Helen E Urquhart

SCOTLAND (BANNOCKBURN)

We used to get a special treat,
The baker's van came down our street,
Iced buns - and cookies, take your pick
'Eat them slowly, don't be sick.'
Life was safe without a care.
Mum and Dad always there.
At night the coalfire gave us heat,
Mum toasted marshmallows for a treat,
Life must have been harder then,
Daily tasks never at an end.
No fancy washing machines and the like
Clothes dried on the pulley at night.
Before I go completely off track.
My thoughts to bring right back.
Now older, I've had my chance to see,
Some of the world and be free.
To see life in different ways.
But there's no place on earth -
I'd rather stay.

Ruth Newlands

THE DARK TRADE

On the ropes
This dark trade
Punch-drunk and forlorn;
Down for the count
This dark trade
Boxing Babylon.

Money, myth, betrayal
Has tolled the final bell;
Blood season on the canvas
Black lights caught in hell.

Fire and fear
This dark trade
Fated crown of thorns;
And another pug
With slurred words
The dollar does not mourn.

John Dewar

ABERDEENSHIRE

Living in the city
I feel a wanderlust
To visit greener pastures
And Banchory is a must

You have the river Feugh
Where you see the salmon leaping
Surrounded with awesome scenery
To lock in your memory for keeping

Banchory offers everything
From a picnic to a banquet
Luscious green pastures
Or the heather clad mountains

You need not travel far
From this Scottish haven
The feeling of tranquillity
It must be close to heaven

The hospitality of the people
Gives a sense of belonging
And on returning home
I experience a sense of longing.

Caroline Robertson

GEORDIE'S NEW SHOES

Gan canny where yer gannin
With new skeets upon yer feet
'Cos the ticket man's a comin
Tappy lappy doon the street

Aan aah can't afford to pay him
This week he's gettin noot
'Cos the scullery floor wants diyin
Aav te buy the tarry toot

So divint scuff yer new skeets
'Cos they'll have te gan te hock
Unless there's oot agannin
Doon aalang the dock

So gan canny where yer gannin
Mind yer Ps and Qs
And what ivvor ye are diyin
Take care them bloody shoes.

A I Graham

MY SHETLAND VIEW

Bright wind-beaten flowers, standing where they freeze,
Fresh green grass, blowing with the breeze,
Vast, vital sea, holding creatures all year round,
Dull thick cloud, so as the sun cannot be found,
Lonely isolated lighthouse, warning ships - *beware!*
Peaceful, blue loch, getting higher with the tide,
Pretty hazel-coloured foals, running in the field, vast and wide.
Bouncing, grey rabbits, hopping frantically around,
High dangerous cliffs of Fetlar, rising out of the ground.
Loud, noisy seagulls, having a 'seagull' race,
Old, but interesting standing stone, standing proudly in its place.

Catriona M M Ferguson (12)

TELEGRAPH HILL

Darkness all around us,
and a silence so loud it's bursting,
save for that distant hum that is soon ignored.
We walk together with anticipation to impel us,
through a belt of trees; beech, birch, ash, hazel - who knows?
They offer only their hanging outlines and secrets,
and a communal stirring from a breeze.
As if themselves conferring on these strangers
walking through their shadowy embrace.

Out of the woods now - climbing, climbing!
A summit is waiting. A view! A rest!
Summer night air mingles with gentle laughter,
how easy an ascent with a distracted mind!
This once site of a signalling tower,
sending its Waterloo messages,
now here for us in this time,
a stage for a play we are writing.

On Telegraph Hill, they are all out tonight,
sprinkled on this concave dome above our heads.
We are caught up in this jumble of stars,
reflecting our insignificance.
Showing us enormity through wide, blinking eyes.

On Telegraph Hill as we lay there together,
I realise this distance is my burden, my choice.
So I slip my hand to yours, as we gaze to the heavens.
And as your fingers grip tightly my fear slips away.
You are the stars tonight.
And the night revolves around us on Telegraph Hill.

Carl D Henderson

LUTON ALAS

Once leafy lanes and shopless roads,
Rabbits playing, frogs and toads,
Peace and calm, and country air,
Green, green grass, and time to spare,
My mind drifts back to cottage thatched,
To youngsters playing, trousers patched,
Of country life that once survived,
Before the traffic jams arrived,
To theatres standing tall and proud,
Once entertained that long lost crowd,
For market stalls that then were real,
Heaped with goodies, us to fill,
The milkman with his horse and cart,
A worker on an early start,
But Luton's changed, it's all a rush,
Traffic creeping in a crush,
Houses! Flats! They build and build,
No wonder that the country's killed,
By all those fumes from flashy cars,
And chimney smoke blots out the stars.
Luton's centre's filled with covered shops,
With car parks all along rooftops.
I can remember back to no M1,
what ever has this country done.
At night no more you walk alone,
For that's the time that muggers roam.
I! Just find it makes me sad,
After all those real good times I had.
Well! That's progress, so they say,
We live to fight another day.

J Bright

RETIREMENT FREEDOM IN BEDFORDSHIRE

To wander down blackberry lane
From madding crowds, feel sane,
Freedom from vandals dirty
Who sacrilege nature's beauty
To rise when dew is still on grass
And through those glorious cobwebs pass
To see the sun first peep at dawn
To feel so glad that I was born
Breathing morning air so fresh
And watch while nature change her dress
First a misty grey and blue
Then rapidly transform the hue
To gold and green, and orange bright
Oh! I would not miss this morning light
And so each age has its advantages
Free to look, no struggle now for my wages.
To seek peace, and not revenge, it's hard but wins in the end,
To seek pleasures here at home, not be deceived and start to roam
To truly value what is good, not put your love in gold or wood
These are only material things, only *care* when a child sings
To bed anytime, even nine, or stay up late long past bedtime
To stare through bedroom window dark
In blackest velvet, stars are marked
Streetlights yellow send their glow, to lonely people comfort show
Free to watch the cars whiz by, and wonder where they go? And why?
Freedom! The whole world would steal, and scoffers at our
                                        prayers we kneel
But we are free to chose and love, no forced love is ever enough
And *once you believe*, there is *no doubt*, all other loves we
                                        can do without

Free to thank for freedom's choice!
Oh! To be free! We all rejoice! Because we are!

Millicent B Colwell

BEDFORDSHIRE

Bedfordshire
A greener place than I have seen
Than many places I have been
A happy playground everywhere
With children's laughter in the air
The hills and trees and farmers' lands
With many things to pick with hands.

O Bedfordshire has been for me
The place that's always gonna be
The land I've lived
The land I've loved
My days began here from the start
My life's been lost
My life's been found
My feet are always on the ground.

O Bedfordshire I feel you
When in some distant land
I never shall forget it's you
The place where I began.

John George Kinsella

GOING HOME

I'd like to go back where I belong,
To the city where I was born,
Glasgow was the place to be,
Lots to do and lots to see,
Growing up having fun,
Playing in the summer sun.

When I married we moved away,
Dingwall's now where I stay,
A small town, but very pretty,
It's not a patch on Glasgow city.

Here I sit on my own,
Longing to go home,
Back to Glasgow where I belong.

Agnes Robertson

FISHING FIFE COAST

The clear August sky
Clouds flowing by, on easterly breeze
Crests of the waves, flowing so calm
Touching the shoreline, with a massive slam
Breaking up stones and pebbles alike
Rods standing still
Like the crest of one's hill
Far in the distance against the back drop
The remnants of what was the man of the rock
Rocks jutting outwards from the cliff top
Rod flickers downwards, then standing still
Only the motion of underground spills
How small I do feel
Under this deep blue sky
Tightening my reel, as the seagulls fly by
Standing upon rocks
Which were once underground
The pits dug them up, scattered them all around
In search of the black rock
Our old fosseled friend
Without these I feel, I would be standing on sand
Instead of raised land
Rod tip still still.

Gary Ritchie

BEDFORDSHIRE COUNTY

If you look round our county,
You'd be surprised at the amount
Of fascinating things there are,
Far more than you can count.

All my long life I've lived in
The county of Bedfordshire,
And scattered in its boundaries,
Are the things I hold most dear.

Animals at Whipsnade zoo,
Have roamed there for many years,
And given lots of pleasure,
Despite people's earlier fears.

The river Ouse which runs through
A lot of the countryside,
Plays host to many regattas,
Because it's so very wide.

Some of the many stately homes,
Which in this district abound,
Are Luton Hoo, Putteridge, and Woburn,
Others can also be found.

Looking out over the downs,
With the gliders flying free,
You get a really lovely view,
As far as the eye can see.

And when you want to travel,
To places both far and near,
You don't go far to start your trip,
As Luton airport is here.

Isobel Crumley

BEAMS FROM FRASERBURGH

Beams sent out for fifteen miles
Towards ships in the North Sea
Oiled by whales and petrol fumes
From eighteen eighty-seven the castle grew
To flash those beams through ocean's firth
Twelve a minute kept men on earth

Worked at height by weighted clock
Down the lighthouse's shafted block
Light reflected first then beamed
Through layers of lenses made supreme
Engineers pierced misty air for lives
Windswept stretch the Broch's own miles

Now beside its newer light
Kinnaird Castle heads the coast
Living as museums do
Buchan's lot that beamed until
Keepers left their charge alone
To computers' caring role

The north's first lighthouse beamed
Over furious seas tamed by names
R L Stevenson's forebears strived
Lit seas akin to modern times
Keeping afloat men's ships with zeal
Scotland's Lighthouse Museum reveals.

David A Bennett

ROUKEN GLEN

Will you come to Rouken Glen, bonnie laddie, oh.
Let us wander once again, bonnie laddie, oh.
   Through the woods where trees so tall
Shade the burn whose gentle call,
   To the entrancing waterfall
         Where we linger, oh.

To the High Park we will go, bonnie laddie, oh.
Past the pond where children row, bonnie laddie, oh.
   To the fields that gently fall,
Where we played with bat and ball,
   Till the gloaming shadowed all,
         Happy memories, oh.

Past the rocky hollow place, bonnie laddie, oh.
Where the Highland cattle graze, bonnie laddie, oh.
   Standing still with gaze serene,
Russet coats amid the green,
   And the blue sky lights the scene,
         Peace abiding, oh.

See it all in summer's pride, bonnie laddie, oh.
Or in sparkling wintertide, bonnie laddie, oh.
   But in autumn best of all,
Glorious in September fall,
   Leaves of flame and gold enthral.
         The Glen is magic, oh!

Margaret M Osoba

MY HOME COUNTY IN SCOTLAND

The place I was born recently changed name
From Banffshire to Moray District a quiet county
Mostly farming area with fields of potatoes and corn
Cattle, pig farming and sheep so forlorn also shooting game
Eventually with hard graft comes the bounty.
Fishing is also a very popular sport
But really quite expensive
Shoals to import and shoals to export
Salmon are definitely more defensive
Than haddock scaly herring and cod
Caught in nets and abundant
Trout too are hooked privately by rod
Food for which the people are dependant
Summer climate is moderate
Winter can be very harsh
Sometimes early other times late
Take your wellies or you might get stuck in the marsh

Distilleries also play a big part
Producing whiskies for the local pub
For farmers to bid with confidence at the local mart
To supply hotels with meat for fine grub
Chicken too is a favourite dish
Bred for every table
Leave the breast bone for a wish
After cuisine a tale or a fable
Jumpers and cardigans made in woollen mills
Various colours and styles warm
For shopping sightseeing or romping over craggy hills
Maybe working on a blizzard down on the farm.

Ann Copland

Proud To Be A 'Quine'

Aberdeen, my home town
I am proud of my origin
An being an Aberdonian
But not living there, makes me frown.

I miss my home town, Aberdeen
Where I feel that I belong
Walking through the crowded streets
Where accents sound like a familiar song.

My own accent still has the twang
Of Aberdonian in my lungs
Appearing when my temper bangs
Elongated vowels rattling off my tongue.

Most of my relatives are in Grampian area
Where as I am living in Perthshire
Scenic Perthshire and 'berry fields
Tourists and farmers everywhere to be seen.

Maybe one day, I might return
To my most favourite town
Staying in Perthshire has its moments
Being proud of heritage is more important.

Diane Simpson

Scotland's Gifts

I've sat in beauty, bathed by the rain
Walked out in the darkness
Blessed sunshines rays

I've stepped in green fields of growing corn
Lay down in the forest
My soul reborn

The snow white beaches, my favourite place
Cleared by high tides
Washed by the waves

Hillsides of flowers, a land in bloom
The heartbreaking splendour
Heals every wound

Lynn McCloskey

SCOTTISH HERITAGE

To start a new year, with a brand new song,
About this lovely land, where I belong,
It's just an island surrounded by sea,
It means more than the world to me,
If you go up North you'll see,
The lovely hills and glens
It's an artists dream the way the colours blend,
To see this Islands historical castles,
That tell the tale of forgotten battles,
In all the world, she rules supreme,
This lovely land ruled by our Queen.
How my heart fills up when I hear the bagpipes play,
Or to see the kilty swinging on his way,
The mighty rivers running out to sea.
The lakes and lochs, a splendour to see,
I'm a Scot and I'm proud you know,
Of this lovely land that I love so,
All of this I have at hand on this lovely Isle of Scotland,
All of this God gave to me on the day that I was born,
No other gift could be as grand,
As a Scottish heritage to this lovely land.

Evelyn Adam

THE COUNTRYSIDE OF FIFE

Upon the countryside of Fife the sun rose,
A landscape of features many did light reveal,
Awakening a vision of great detail and beauty immense,
That darkness had made sleep.
A patchwork of fields delighted on lights arrival,
Some of which waved in flowing jubilation,
Perhaps like an abstract sea.
Also upon a forest,
Where firs stood proudly tall,
A slanting light arrived,
Revealing shapes and Scottish colours,
That to the open eye, amazement brought.
Water too did the sunrise excite,
The burn that earlier trickled, the light now made run.
Upon a distant hill too, with a shimmering loch in its lap,
Did light pour proudly.
Creatures too the rising sun did not forget,
A pheasant, fluttering playfully, danced as the tickling sunlight spread,
Sheep and cows also, walked in sprightly fashion,
Amongst rodents too did happiness reign,
With eyes wide and smiling faces, they explored their habitat.
Also upon the chequered landscape floor,
Yawning farmhouses stretched,
As yellow light had made slumber cease.
From their windows, faces peered out,
Viewing the painted scene of overflowing colour and depth,
That before this day, upon such beauty I had never gazed,
Until this day, the day the sun rose,
On the countryside of Fife.

Paul A Smith

KIRKCALDY IN FIFE

Born and bred in the county of Fife,
I married an Irishman and became his wife.
We live in Kirkcaldy a beautiful town,
With its seashore and landscapes a pleasure unfound.
We live at the seaside just up from the shore,
With a rose coloured garden and a bright red door.
The scene is beautiful you'd have to see,
If you're passing by come in and see me.

The Ravenscraig castle is a landmark to see,
The historic ruins lie up from the sea.
Across from the castle there's a great place to be,
The Ravenscraig park brings memories to me.
On the family day's outing we had fun and games,
My sister and I and our big brother James.
We'd play on the swings and we'd feed the ducks,
Then we'd go home all covered in muck.

Another attraction take it from me,
Is Kirkcaldy Links market down by the sea.
An annual event it costs a packet,
Centuries old it's such a racket.
Thousands gather from all over Fife,
For this week long carnival (what a life)
The kids look forward with sheer delight,
To the age old carnival colourful and bright.

So if you're ever near Fife come in and see,
And sit yourself down to a nice cup of tea.
The people are warm, pleasant and kind,
With a friendly manner it's simply divine.
Given a choice of where I should be,
Is Kirkcaldy in Fife down by the sea.

Lou

THE VILLAGE

Upon the hill I sit and stare,
And think of all that I've done there,
Of how days used to be,
In this village that's been good to me.

Memories turning in my head,
Kinglassie I am born and bred,
Folks, the salt of the earth kind,
Acts of kindness running in my mind.

The roads black with men in line,
Wending their way to pit and mine,
To work all day in the dark,
No glimmer of light not even a spark.

And now these days are gone,
A different road we are walking on,
But still a village I do see,
That's been good to me.

Generations have gone to that school,
To learn to live to its rule,
Many have left its roots,
To return again with younger shoots.

It is the folk that is its heart,
Each one doing their part,
To see that it will never die,
It will live on for you and I.

Yes I sit a while and stare,
And think of folk who really care,
About the village that I see,
A village that's been good to me.

Agnes Kirk

BANFF

Perhaps it's the sun setting over the sea
Or the tranquillity that appeals to me
Banff, the place that stole my heart
And keeps it safe while we're apart

When I first arrived on that cold winter's day
And stood windswept, looking over the bay
A total stranger, in a strange place
I cried, the tears running down my face

But the tears soon dried and I started smiling
As I found the place and the people beguiling
I was warmly welcomed with open arms
Won over completely by their charms

Promotion lured me back to the city
And I blindly accepted, more's the pity
I left the place I love the most
That beautiful town on the north-east coast

I've travelled across the world and back
On highways and off the beaten track
But nowhere is the sky as bright
As Banff, on a balmy summer's night

Soon I'll go back to the people I love
To the prettiest town under heaven above
I'll walk on the beach looking over the bay
Home at last, and this time I'll stay.

Elizabeth Cameron

SCOTLAND THE BRAVE

The Highland clans, wi' tartans a'
wi' kilts and sporrans and spats and a'
wi' plyds and frills and bonnets braw
   sae grand tae see.
Wi' drums abeat and pipes ablaw
   they fair thrill me.

When on the march I see them come,
to skirl o' pipes or tuck o' drum,
it's then my soul and I become
   with joy possessed,
and my proud heart beats like a drum,
   within my breast.

Music hath charms, ah ken it weel,
the sound of pipes and drums I feel,
provide the charm that's bound to steal
   your hert away,
the rhythm fits the tunes sae weel,
   ye swing and sway.

Such fun, such joy, the tunes reveal,
two-four, six-eight, Strathspey or reel,
like magic they can make you feel,
   the urge tae dance,
and you respond to their appeal,
   at every chance.

The lads sae braw, with steps sae gay,
a bonnie sicht, aye, ony day,
three cheers for Scotland and long may
   her standard wave,
long live the tune the pipers play,
   Scotland the Brave.

William MacDonald Hughes

UNTITLED

My home is Scotland, coast to coast,
her towns and cities have been my host.
John O'Groats to the borders her magnificent land,
green hill, white mountain, silver stream, golden sand.
Angus beef, Scottish salmon, whisky tartan and tweeds
stately buildings, great ships, famous people she breeds.
Steeped in history, real heroes, lives ending too soon
Mystical romance and fantasy, like Brig O' Doon.
They come in their thousands from lands far away,
sights to see, game to catch famous courses to play.
Wherever they wander, the best people they'll meet,
be it up ben the castle, or just doon the street.
Born to be Scottish, - blessed with more than my share,
to see all her splendour, - with the travelling fair.

Frances Hiscoe

RENFREWSHIRE

Siding the Clyde
With green entrancing scene
Oak and fir tree height
Part of its century
Of romance and renown
In previous centuries
Fame of sacred site
Ancient castle and abbey
Old cotton mill
Airport in early days of flying
Large ferry and recent massive bridge
Though in vicinity of major city
Retaining a detached tranquillity.

G McKewn

UNTITLED

Wallace, Bruce and the Celtic Kings,
Mackintosh genius and beautiful things,
Sweeping glens, mountain tops,
Discovering the beauty never stops.

Prickly thistles, gorse and nettles,
Rainbow palette of flowers and petals,
Bluebells, sea shells, men in kilts,
Bagpipes, haggis, whisky stills.

Heather cushions on knobbly knolls
Leading to dances in ceilidh halls
With cheery greetings from cheery people
Expressing talents with mods and fiddle.

Jet-skiing, fishing, rambling, climbs,
Picking fruit - happy times,
Swirling mist, clear blue skies,
Distinctive taste of paradise.

Fragrant blossom, refreshing pine,
Crackling log fires, sweet mulled wine,
The scent of sea-food in the air
As creels and nets deliver with flair.

Smooth golden sand, black ragged rocks,
Cliffs and crags, eagles and hawks,
Castles, caves, waterfalls,
Mountain stag, cruachan calls.

Sheep farm, fish farm, cattle and crops,
Curving seashore, rivers and lochs,
Long and deep, blue, dark and fresh,
'Rest and be thankful' in the great Northwest!

Eva Goldstein

THE GRAND TOUR OF FIFE

Over the Forth on to the Tay
A lot to see along the way
The silver sands of Aberdour
Children playing by the hour
Alexander rode through a raging storm
Went over the cliff top at Kinghorn.
Robinson Crusoe by Daniel Defoe
Looks out from a niche in Lower Largo
If you can hit a hole in one
Stop at St Andrews for some fun.

Newport stands on the River Tay
Where steel and concrete cross the way
By Normans Law to Cupar go
The county town of Fife you know
On to Lindores with a fishing rod
And Auchtermuchtys down the road
Past the Howe with pastures green
Producing crops for folk to glean
Steeped in history from the past
Falkland Palace has the cast

Up the Lomond, over the hill
Where gliders fly if it's not too still
Down to Lochgelly and Cowdenbeath
Skilled miners hued deep underneath
The nation has preserved old Culross
To make a feature for the tourist
Rosyth a defunct naval base
Will electronics take its place?
Fife is a Kingdom on its own
That's why I'm proud to call it home.

Maureen Glennie

JUST VISITING

Hear the piper play his song
Honking at the passing throng
Irish pubs with Gaelic names
International Highland games
Little grannies in their kilts
'Excuse me' with Greenock lilts
Ugly ladies with bad hair
Dance reels to a Scottish air.

Some men do not like to roam
In the Edinburgh gloam
But I always feel at home
As an Englishman in Scotland.

Jammed up vans like bees in jars
Drivers smiling from their cars
Yanks are looking for their roots
Under roofs like onion shoots
Streets that modern time forgot
Listed buildings left to rot
Tourists stroll through ruined rubble
Past the kids who look for trouble
Kicking trash along the lane
Skinny as a weather vein.

Sometimes I look underfed
Bony on my cardboard bed
But I never lose my head
As an Englishman in Scotland.

On the skyline, see the hills!
Cure for all those rain-soaked ills
Rugged coast for soft-heart folk
Calling to the rich and broke
Fresh air from a purple sky
Ringing with a battle cry
Sod the neighbours, shout it loud -
I'm a visitor and proud!

Wandering down a mountain pass
Through the heather and the grass
I forget my place and class
An Englishman in Scotland.

Nick Smith

ABERDEEN: FROM A DISTANCE

You awake and I can sense the sun glisten on your countenance
Eyes open now, I reach out to embrace you
And smell you
And touch you
And bask in your atmosphere

I have stripped you bare in my mind's eye
And I have seen you resplendent in rich brocade

Yes, there is the shimmering grey granite
The wild, unkempt, sea spilling onto the shore
The lush greenery, the perfumed flowers
The ancient, cobbled, streets sitting shyly in the shade of
the nineties shopping malls
The imposing office blocks jutting out proudly from the row
of terraced houses
The unploughed fields and the furrows of endeavour

But most of all there is the warmth you exude
Glowing on a cold winter's day
Listening quietly to your people
Their tales of Northeast life
The latest page of your story.

Gordon T Walker

KIRKCALDY

Thank you for taking me into your heart,
For opening up my eyes
And giving me sight to find my bearings again.
Thank you for bathing me in your beauty.
You made me feel at home.
You made me feel whole again in Kirkcaldy.

Your rolling seas
Took away my tears
And calmed my fears.
Your soothing breeze
Kept my secrets safe.
I feel privileged to have seen your world.

It's unlikely I'll ever get back this way
But your image will with me forever stay.
Thank you for the space to breathe
And for healing time.
It was here I found the strength
To lay some ghosts to rest.
A part of me remains forever with you.

Fond farewell, fond adieu
I'll always remember my time with you.
You've made me feel so welcome
That I've come to think of you
As my home away from home.
With your kind permission
I'll tell others too,
That the lost can find their way back home;
Via Kirkcaldy.

Maxx Maynard

KIRKLAND GAIRDINS

Oh, Kirkland Gairdens, when we were wee
Wis sic a place for fun an' glee!
D'ye min' fitbaw games on summer nights?
Levoi, Tig an' Bonfire fights?
The favourite haunts fur us tae meet
Wis Kirkland Walk an' Byron Street;
While Jack Wakefield's tae the Sullivan's place
Wis jist the length tae run a race.

On Methil Brae stood twa auld grey schools
Where we a' learned a few golden rules:
An neither Martin, McSheffrey nor auld Miss Stoat,
Sparerd the tawse on dunce or classroom goat.

Then after school, doon the Dam - the fun wis great
Walkin' ower the big black pipe . . .an' temptin' fate:
D'ye min the fifteen-a-side ower the Gairdens park?
An fleein' up the 'Pen' fur chips when it wis dark?

Doon Linton's sawmill . . . we'd never tire -
O' runnin' like hell, when the place 'caught' fire.
An Rosie Black, 'Guid-Time' Gail, an Mo, ower the Coup
Wid tak it in turns 'tae loup' the sturdy upright fences.

Roddy McKee the baker, then wis slow bit sure
His auld Clydesdale walkin' roon the gairdens; four miles an oor.
His horse an' cairt wid amble by -
Fresh baked bread and dung - fur the Gairdens; Roddy wid cry!

An in those days the Gairdens hid a team
When the likes O'Brian, Tosh and Tam broch't it fame:
Kin ye jist imagine a' their faces noo?
If the video camera hid been aroond tae capture that view?

Still - in spite o' it a' - some things *will* last -
We'll aye dream o' the Gairdens o' oor treasured past.

Dominic Currie

A 'HEARTY' JAUNT

The West Highland Way - the adventure is on
For Willie and Eddie and Alex and Don.
They're all kitted out and they've got all the gear
But most important of all - Cath and Charlie are here.

So they've started their training - in sunshine and rain,
A quick stop for coffee, then onwards again.
But mind - it's a walk - it's not a race
As Charlie would say - 'All at your own pace.'

This super-fit team - are they athletes of note?
When they complete the course, they'll have reason to gloat,
The Olympics will wonder - 'Are they *Golds* from the past'?
Not on your life - that's the *Healthy Hearts* class!

The training was over - the real thing was here
But with Charlie and Cath there - they'd nothing to fear.
The rain - how it poured from a dark cloudy sky
As the Healthy Hearts Club started out from Milngavie.

Some slept in a wigwam, some slept in a tent
In a bunkhouse and hostel on this great event.
The day walkers came, then went home to their bed
But the stalwart nineteen just kept forging ahead.

With their tums full of pasta - their healthy hearts gay
Who would have believed that they'd walk 'The Way'.
A tribute indeed to our own SRI
To the staff and their care as these dark days dragged by.

But they've done it - they're home - the achievement is great.
A bond has been forged - each one is a mate.
And Catherine and Charlie can both proudly say
'We got them fit - for the West Highland Way.'

Margaret J Paton

112

SWEET GLEN LONAN

There's a wee glen in Argyleshire
There's a sweet glen in the west
It's the spot of scenic beauty
It's the place that we love best
Be it rain or let the sun shine
It is there we love to bide
In our caravans in comfort
Nestling closely side by side

We come back in the springtime
When the lambs are frisking free
Where the hovering of the eagle
Is a wondrous sight to see
Also in the summertime
When the hills are purply green
And the tourists come once more to see
Their own dear glen of dreams

In autumn-time again we come
To listen to the sound
Of calling birds and bleating lambs
And all creatures of the ground
Who fill our hearts again with joy
Like the gospel bells do chime
Before the coming once again
Of the cold bleak wintertime

Now that winter's here again
And the hills are white with snow
The flocks are safely gathered
In the valley down below
Carefully tended by their shepherds
Throughout the winter drear
Until the buds do sprout again
Then we know that spring is here.

Pat McLaughlin

BORDERS OF SCOTLAND

My eyes now roam the border hills
Where my feet no longer go
Their beauty haunts the heart still
It's there that tells me so
Purple heather is alive once more
Across the old drove road
September blooms o'er border moors
Water wallflowers in their scores
Purple sheen across hill tops
When the sun glints in the sky
The dew, it sparkles at early morn
It tells the season why
The border hills are home to me
In this, my Scottish home
My eyes still wander, they can see
So much beauty
You can never be alone

Janet L Murray

TO A LOCHABER WILDCAT

Wild, wilful, wandering:
The cold milk of the moon in your veins,
In your belly the fire of the sun.
Sharp as the claw of winter,
Fearless as spring,
Dappled by summer clouds,
Thistledown fall,
Hard as the boulders' shelter,
Wild through the centuries,
Molten with the vent of the earth;
Snarl then as you pass,
Like the wind on grass.

E J Macdonald

WHAT IS MY SCOTLAND?

This is my Scotland.
Scenic views, Scotch whisky and sweet shortbread,
  Historic Scone, home to the Stone of Destiny.
Cairngorms, clans, contagious Clootie-dumpling,
  The corries, reels and Highland dancing at the Ceilidh.
Ochils, oatcakes, Outer Isles by ferry, sailing from Oban,
  Taste the rich ochre of cheese from Orkney.
Turnberry - golf, Tattoo, tartan, tasty sticky toffee,
  Flowing salmon waters of the Tweed and Tay.
Lamas Fair, Largs, lochs, language of the Gaels,
  A lone piper's lament by the shores of Loch Fyne.
Alba, Arbroath smokies, perlusive auld reekie,
  Hogmanay, voices singing Auld Lang Syne.
Nairn, Newport, Nigg, notorious Nessie, newspapers,
  New hope for the future and the Northern Lights.
Dunoon, Dunkeld, Dunfermline, Scot's discovery,
  A daring dram, afore ye go, Dundee cake a delicious delight.

Yvonne Fraser

SPRING EVENT

It is another sign of spring, when the Langtoun light's up.
Wagons roll well into the night and chaos reigns supreme,
As traffic is diverted to extremes.
On the prom, Linktown dwellers are poised for the intrusion,
On their peace and privacy for the six day duration.
Only the weather that this phenomenon brings, belies the spring,
As winter always returns for one last fling.
But overall, it is our main annual event of the year.
People come from far and near, as they have done throughout the years
To visit Kirkcaldy's own longest famous open fair,
The *Links Market,* in our Langtoun . . .

Agnes L W Berry

SCOTLAND

They say the grass is greener,
On the other side.
But I've not found that true
Though I've searched far and wide.
But I've not found that true,
To me there's no land fairer,
Than the one in which I live.
Nowhere could you find such wealth,
Than what Scotland has to give.

Its rich and rugged mountains,
Its rivers and its streams.
The peace within its glens,
Where one can sit and dream.
To walk among the heather,
See the new born lambs in spring.
And the warmth of the Scottish people,
Makes your heart want to sing.

To watch the majestic eagle,
Soaring through the sky,
Hear the haunting strain of the bagpipes,
Lifting spirits high.
See the graceful Scottish dancers,
As they dance the highland fling.
And the beauty of its islands,
Touched with a breath of spring.

Watch the tossing of the caber,
Or the women as they weave.
And once you've seen o'er Scotland,
You'll not want to leave.
For you could fly to Paris.
To New York or to Rome.
But none would be more beautiful,
Than the land I call my home.

M Muirhead

THE WELSH GIANT

When I was young I loved to study maps.
Atlas at hand, I'd climb on Grandma's lap.
Now she was Welsh, so we would look at Wales.
Of myths and legends she would me regale.
Of Merlin, dragons, stories of the past.
Of how the great Welsh Giant stones would cast
From Snowdon, throwing them far out to sea.

The Giant's head in hat was Anglesey.
Caernarfon was his arm pointing to sea.
And Denbigh was the rucksack or his pack
With Flint . . . the large stone carried on his back.
Unbuttoned . . . Merioneth . . . Welsh wool coat.
I thought the Giant pointed to a boat,
But Grandma said 'St George's Channel . . . see?'

With right leg . . . Cardigan . . . he strode along.
In . . . Pembroke and Carmarthen . . . boots so strong.
Montgomery . . . an extra sack of stones.
His left leg . . . Radnor, Brecknock . . . made him groan,
Because . . . Glamorgan . . . his left boot did lack
Toe-part . . . was missing . . . he had dropped the sack
Of stones upon his foot one stormy day.

To stop the pain he dipped boot-toe in sea.
Still hear him roar and groan when storms there be.
Offa built a dyke 'gainst the English foes.
We walked it once, but that was long ago.
This was the way I loved to study maps.
I could see the Giant safe in Grandma's lap.
I treasure all her tales of long ago.

Elwynne

CULROSS

The village time
Almost forgot
The little houses
Where people abide
So peaceful
Under star lit sky
The abbey protects
Looking down
From above
Culross the village
I dearly love
The quiet walks
During the day
The type of village
Where gentle people stay
The spring gardens
When in full bloom
The tourists come
To view
Culross I love you

Robert Mercer

THE HIGHLANDS

From tiny blades of grass so green, to heather, gorse and broom,
From moors to hills to mountains high, and valleys dark and gloom,
To streams and rivers flowing, to lochs in valleys bare,
These things make up the Highlands, and for these us Scots we care.

When rain pours from the heavens, in sheets blown by the wind,
This land we call the Highlands, can look very, very grim,
The mountains black the lochs so grey, the sky as dark can be,
Makes barren crags and woodlands dark, a sight that you must see.

Now when the sun it shines from high, great changes you will see,
It's as though a magic wand were waved, to set the beauty free,
The mountains high are bathed in sun, the eerie gloom is shed,
The streams and lochs they glitter, as from mountains high they're fed.

The heather blooms and grasses grow, there are many shades of green,
Even pines and silver birch their beauty must be seen,
There is nothing like the Highlands, so tranquil and so free,
There is no place like the Highlands, that I would rather be.

Marjory Davidson

SIMPLY PONDERING!

Why ever do fish wriggle
When it's said they feel no pain
Could it be for a giggle
Knowing they'll be hooked again.

A goldfish on the other hand
is happy in a bowl,
Not for it the sea nor sand
Where anglers take their toll.

To say that all fish cannot fly
Would be a bit absurd
I wouldn't want to be a fry,
I'd rather be a bird.

It's calm and tranquil by the Loch
perhaps I'll catch the Monster,
A tiddler would be such a mock
I'd settle for a lobster.

I'm glad being just as I am
neither rich nor poor.
Just a common fisherman
with my tempting lure.

Alexander Buchanan

THE LAND OF SCOTS

Standing amidst a utopia
The sweet scent of heather captures my breath,
And the bitter taste of salt lines my lips.
Awed by the elegant gusts of wind,
Which sweep the undulating hills,
I stand motionless.

The vast blueness is unable to retain the mountains,
Which tower over me like gods
And beyond the soft whistling of the fields of thistles,
I hear the distant shout of battle cries
The clash of steel and the crisp clink of swords
Back to a time where bravehearts died for her

Sudden subdued realisation grips my mind,
As whispers of freedom surround me.
Scared in the hearts of Scots,
And requisite for their land
Liberty will always reside eternally within her.

Ashwin Kher

NOT HOME

Wales is home
because
it's
where
My Mum and Dad
live.

I'm glad I've got
this
sort of
home.

Mary Drayton

A BATHGATE BAIRN

Bathgate was the birthplace of
Sir James Young Simpson
Who was born 185 years ago
And became Bathgate's most famous son.

He stayed in Bathgate until he was
The tender age of fourteen
Before going to Edinburgh University
Becoming a surgeon aged eighteen.

Though a qualified surgeon
Too young for his degree in medicine
He tried to find work on the ships
But even they would not employ him.

Disappointed and short of money
Simpson had to wait
He started delivering bread again
As he had once done in Bathgate.

But life eventually forged ahead
Simpson obtained his degree in 1832
Fifteen years later he discovered chloroform
Which is now very important to me and you.

For it is used as an anaesthetic
In hospitals all over, every day
Helping to make surgery safer
In every possible way.

Returning in 1861, roots never forgotten
Simpson invited girls at Bathgate Academy
To compete for a silver thimble
Given to him by his faithful sister, Mary.

Ian Fowler

RIVER FORTH ROCK

As long as there's a rocking chair on a Dysant
Share, set it rock forever more.
There's nothing new under the sun.
The best pop and rock has already been sung.
Rock stars will shine on and on . . .
Long after we are dead and gone.

As long as there's a guitar on a Fife shore,
There will be rock forever more.

Come pick the mumbling bass.
Let's clash the splashing cymbals,
Then shout at Mike with those gritty vocals.
Bring in the chord changes on the rhythm guitar,
And carry the message loud and far.

As long as there's a bass on the Bass Rock,
Rock 'n' roll will never stop.

You've brought your well-worn records.
I've bought some great CDs.
As you switched on, we were turned on
 - As though The Band were playing in our front room.

As long as there's a rock and bap on a crail shore,
There'll be rock 'n' roll forever more.

In the beginning rock was derided.
'The Youth will be corrupted by the devil's music'.
Its critics hoped and prayed - it wouldn't last long,
But like the healthiest Heartbeat, it's still going strong.

Mark Young

MEMORIES OF OLD DERBY

It's pre-war Derby I like to recall,
The dear old theatre, Empire and White Hall.
The *Palais de Dance,* and after the ball!
Boots on the corner, Edgar Horne in the Strand
The Arboretum, host to the visiting band.
Sol Lux and the Fifty Bob Tailors were there
And Thurman and Malins renowned for their care.
Always of interest and magic to me
At Johnson's the jewellers (come on, it's free)
Was the Gold Ball that dropped at 12 GMT
Williamson's cake shop in busy East Street,
Cream horns at tuppence! Gosh what a treat!
Mr Russell sold fish from his spotless white stall
While *Mid Drapes* Magnet looked down on us all,
When we went to the shops (no trolleys to curse)
We talked of the weather and 'Is Florrie worse?'
Mr Goddard made Bass and Bassine brooms
A skilful man in his Sadler Gate rooms.
Remember the tramcars, three ha'pence the fare
From centre of Derby to 'Ay up, we're there.'
We danced at the Plaza, Sam Ramsden was there,
With Rolls Royce and carnation (some elegance there)
In Friar Gate, that saintly place
(Did friars pray on bended knee?)
A painted sign for all to see
'Drink Copestake's delicious Friary Tea.'
Those aromatic shops we knew
Soon all will have passed away,
But the *Ram* and *Fountain* are here to stay,
With Bonnie Prince Charlie 'statued' on his charger,
He came to Derby, cried 'About turn, no further!'
Behold a modern turn around,
The Rams have left the baseball ground!

G Nicklin

BURNS OF SCOTLAND

There was a famous poet by the name of Robbie Burns,
He also worked on the land, doing jobs in turn,
Doing his corresponding up and down the land,
Writing all his famous poems in his own hand,
Mingling with the upper crust of fine gentlemen,
His poems were of bonnie lasses up and down the glen,
Rabbie loved it in his local for a jar now and then,
Telling yarns and reciting all his tales of woe,
How he bantered of days long-long-ago,
The earthing floor was in the home,
Sooter Johnnie with him he did roam,
Tam-o'-shanter Burns thought great,
Rabbie chose him for a special mate,
Burns had only a short life,
He left a family and a wife,
His poems and name still live on.
After two hundred years have gone,
The young handsome laddie is now at rest,
So all raise your glasses for Robbie,
                              . . . All the Best!

Teresa Walker

SEASONS'S GREETINGS

Ah walkit oot ae mornin',
An' the fields wir turnin' green.
The bonnie spikes o'barley,
Had ge'in' a grouan sheen.

Ah walkit oot ae mornin',
Tae see the gress groun high,
An' tae hear the lavrock singin'
In the clear simmer sky.

124

Ah walkit oot ae mornin',
An' the fields had a' ga'en gowd,
An' the bonnie hieds o'barley
Wir staunin' there sae proud.

Ah walkit oot ae mornin',
An' the fields wir broon an' bare,
An' no' a thing wis movin'
In the cauld an' bitter air.

Kate MacLean

HERE'S TAE US!

Rennie MacIntosh and Robert Burns,
Stephen Campbell and Alasdair Grey,
Throughout history took their turns,
Their masterpieces are here to stay

The Glasgow school and Sir Walter Scott,
For artists and writers we're renowned,
All-in-all we're a creative lot,
Our native talent remains unbound.

From William Wallace to Logie Baird,
Roslin Institute and Donald Dewar,
Where would we be if they had not cared,
Our Scottish voice heard, they will assure.

From John Smith to doctors like Fleming,
Our greatest leaders and scientists,
In their fields they have all been leading,
Ever-growing our achievement lists.

For these reasons we feel Scottish pride,
And having covered present and past,
Our future's riding a changing tide,
I know our boundless talents will last.

S E Malkiewicz

ALBA MO GHRAIDH

My beloved Scotland
   How beautiful you look
Dressed in your autumn coat
   Your richness of colour
Though still the grey tops tower
   And the sky
Like a bright, white light shines.

Green and emerald
   Sepia and red
Your coat of many colours
   Dancing to the river bed
Hurried waters, gurgling and gushing
   Mountains in their splendour
      Imposing.

My eyes see all your beauty
   And marvel at your majesty
And I stand in awe of your bounty
   And my heart overflows
      With love for you.

Suu

WALES 1997

Green green mountains - green green, vales
This magical land, is our country, Wales
Legends and myths, steeped in history
Tales of hobgoblins - remain a mystery.

Always a welcome, in this land of, Queen's gold
We are the flock, that go back, to the fold.
Choirs, sing out loud - arias and hymns
Our heartfelt regret, for all, past sins.

This land of ours, now mourns a death
Diana! You were, our every breath.
Due home that night, you didn't know
That God, was calling you, time to go.

Always remembered, here in these hills
Our country adore - both Harry and Wills
They are your legacy - and part of our lives
One day, hope they take, girls like you, for their wives.

Irene Weldon

DELVE A LITTLE DEEPER

We know who we are:
No identification card is needed,
Only a conscious longing to be known as one who is.
We know what we are:
No special attributes are desired,
Only the warmth and kindred soul of love and understanding.
We know what we can do:
No qualifications are required,
Only dedication, commitment and a passion
To strive forth and achieve against intolerable odds.

Welshness is not a label one becomes in being born there -
It is nurtured and is born from the heart.
We are a strongly creative people
Who suffer for our talents.
We are the downtrodden,
We are the oppressed.
We are also armed with the softest touch and a gentle voice,
A pride which bonds and keeps us together.
We are that consciousness which soars through the hills
And longs to be known as 'Welsh'.

Jay M L Horton

CANVAS VIEWS

As darkening mist surrounded
The damp and lonely moor
We huddled in a leaking tent
And shivered, only sure

That at first light, we'd drearily
Desert our destination
And swap our dripping sleeping bags
For comfy civilisation.

But when we woke next morning
The mist had gone from sight
And heather hills so picturesque
Were radiant and bright.

And where there had been greyness
Unknown, so cold and feared
A bay of seals, so sheltered
Had magically appeared.

The water, deepest turquoise.
The sun was rising high.
The sand was warm and golden
As an eagle circled by.

Yes, Scotland's sights are many
And if paradise is resting
You don't know what tomorrow brings
But contrast's interesting!

Sheena Proff

THE GREEN GLENS OF ANGUS

So dear to the heart, the fresh green glens,
   In the shade of each heather-clad hill,
Where blue rivers leap, thro' deep rocky dens,
   Fast tumbling, then suddenly still.

Cool bracken waves, in the heat of the day,
   Where the chaffinches flit quickly by -
There's patches of daisies, where wee lambs play -
   The white clouds are high, in the sky.

Soon heather grows dim, and bracken, brown -
   Red jewels, adorn the dancing rowan tree,
Keeping low on the moor, the grouse crouch down,
   And late salmon, come from the sea.

Then, o'er the hills, a blanket of snow -
   The winter winds howl thro' the corries.
In each home, in the glens, a fire will glow -
   The herd sees the gleam, and hurries.

The hungry red deer, deserts the heights,
   In muffled days, when the birdsong's rare.
The bark of the fox, pierces thro' the nights -
   The warm beasts, are quiet in the byre.

But, comes a new spring, my glens I'll see -
   I'll be there, when the primroses bloom.
Eager hands will reach out, to welcome me -
   Smiling eyes, will tell me, I'm home.

Elizabeth Harris

UP IN STIRLING TOWN

Standing by the castle, high up above the town,
underneath its ancient walls, just standing, looking down,
you have a sense of history, it's everywhere around,
you feel you're in a different age, walking on hallowed ground.
You can almost feel the presence of people long since gone,
you feel it in the very breeze, before you hurry on.
For here in Stirling Castle, Scotland's history was made,
where intrigue, plot and counterplot, and many a scheme was laid.
From over there, upon that hill, brave Wallace did descend
to fight the English to the death, and Stirling to defend.
'Twas long ago - but - listen - can you not hear it still?
The sound of battle, clash of steel, each side intent - to kill.
'Twas Wallace won the battle, down there, by Stirling Bridge -
his monument stands out so clear, 'gainst the Ochils' noble ridge.
And as you leave the castle, to wander through the town
with its medieval houses, you're oft touched by the gown
of someone from that distant past, just hurrying by -
you almost fancy you can hear a single, gentle sigh.
And walking past the Tolbooth, and down the broad main street,
can you not *see* the market stalls? Hear the sound of many feet?
See the jugglers, the urchins, and the 'stilted men',
pushing, poking, jostling - housewife with living hen?
And as you wander on again, you notice the old Jail,
and *shiver* - what went *on* in there - the 'shades' could tell a tale!
The empty windows of Mar's Wark stand, sightless, looking down -
it looms o'er us, so dark, so stark, indeed it seems to frown!
The Market Cross, the 'Puggy' watches from on high -
(why *is* it called 'The Puggy'? - I really don't know why!)
I'm glad I live in Stirling, I'm glad it is my town,
and - I just love to be in Stirling, at the castle, looking down.

Joyce Hockley

STONE CITY

Don't bother me with moonbeams
Or fluffy lambs.
It's the grey stone I like
Cut by the giant into crags
Sheer and daunting
And the cobbles rocky-riding,
Elegant cut sandstone reflecting
Iron-wrought at sunset,
Quite unexpected phallic stones
Footpath sentinels,
Stepped stone edges on the skyline
Leading up to chimneys,
The castle rock, volcanic spew
Guarding the city
And last of all the Stone of Destiny
That pulses with the nation's heart -
These stones are shouting out
With life and time and Edinburgh.

Anne Marie Connolly

ALL THINGS WERE BEAUTIFUL

Perfect was this world of ours
All men, women, pure to God
Amongst the trees and flowers
Beasts of earth, birds of sky
Now the world was at peace
Nobody is arguing, nobody asks why
Why God made Heaven
The seas, mountains and the sky
All things were beautiful
Everyone was happy, everyone did smile
All was to last forever not just for a while.

Arnold Richard Williams

CYRNIAU NOD

Distant you offer nothing
but a meeting place for sky.
Eyes pass over you
looking for places higher.

Closer you are my heart.
The birthplace of clouds.
Where peat hags loom
from misted gloom
and rotted posts curtsey;
clinging to humming wires.

No one walks over you.
Not even sheep.
But I, am drawn
and feel your magic.

You suck at my boots
pleading me to stay.
One day I will;
lie down, blacken
and nourish
your ancient soil.

Martin Evans

DENBIGHSHIRE

If I close my eyes
And think of Denbighshire
I see sheep on rugged hillsides
A poet to inspire.

I see lush green fields around me
And heathers on the moor,
Wildfowl on the rivers
And gulls on the shore.

All of nature's splendour
Is in this part of Wales,
A haven of tranquillity
Amongst the Denbigh vales.

A J Don

THOUGHTS

Engrossed as it were, in milling thoughts,
My heart cried out to believe in myself,
For self-same confidence over my inner mind.
To put that which it inspires, for all the world to see.
And when on view, my inner soul says 'This is not me.'
Why is it so, that creation from mankind
Is never how one thinks it should be?
Put before the humans, criticised, materialised,
Causing, here and there, a spark of light -
Yet only a glimmer that shows for a while,
Dulls and diminishes as days go by.
When turning to a new and better creative idea-
Slipping into orbit according to one's mind,
Great artists, poets, writers, making fame in turn
Dwelling on their names, I see my name engraved.
Though 'all in the mind' my heart declares,
For never has my work or thoughts brought fame to me or anyone.
What is in my heart, mind and thoughts -
Is not in yours and nobody can make it so.
I turn again within myself and let this pen flow,
To escape, set free and true these thoughts, fantasies and dreams
That they may be clear for you as well as me.

M J Morgan

FLYING OVER GWYNEDD

High, high above the summer-hazy sky
unseen, in seeming-slow and solemn progress
their sound moves from horizon to horizon,
now rumbling-muffled, now loud-booming -
and linking continents.

Low, slow, the little lazy pleasure-planes
drone friendly to and fro, take off and land:
seascape and mountainscape in bird's-eye view
and medieval-castled town.

And still (less often now than once)
killer jets streak screaming overhead
like ravening Harpies; far ahead of their own roar
like deadly spears they whirl into the valley.

Evening comes with clearing skies.
Through depths of space the sun pours down
silent, so silent, so intensely silent:
MC^2 = light and warmth and peace.

Gerry Nussbaum

I HEDD WYN (TO HEDD WYN. THE LATE WELSH POET)

You gouge out the pain from the hollow within me,
Wash down my cheeks with unconscious fire.
Defiant you stand for all I hold sacred,
Singing to Myfanwy with wrenching desire.

Yet you are an actor upon my TV screen,
A puppet of others, compelled to obey.
So why do you move me, oh bard of the valley?
How do I feel and know that which you say?

No longer would I, stumble on blindly,
Crushed by the weight of solitude's toll,
If Ellis, I'd had just a singular moment,
To seek out the guidance of your greater soul.

Kürsté James

THE GLEN OF WEEPING

From Rannoch Moor, to the shores of Loch Leven,
The historic! Magnificent! Pass of Glencoe,
Impresses each one, whatever the season,
And visitors flocking, are filled with great awe.

Through the onslaught of hail and rain, did I wander,
As I followed the 'old road' on foot through the pass,
Crags glittering with waterfalls, filled me with wonder,
And I thought of the people no more there, alas!

'Bidean nam Bian': that high craggy mountain,
The site of the 'massacre' so long ago,
William III was the person who ordered that 'great sin'
And forty poor glenfolk were killed by their foe.

The cause was the failure of Clan Chief, MacIan,
To swear the allegiance, before 'New Year's Day',
And men who were led by Campbell of Glen Lyon,
Burnt homes, and killed all, who came in their way.

Now a monument stands, for that time of great sorrow,
MacDonalds are resting, at peace, in the glen,
As you stand by the cross, you can still feel the horror,
Of that tragic deed, that took place, way back then.

Carol Paterson

WELSH CHILDHOOD

Now I am old I often reminisce
My mind wanders back to my childhood in Wales,
To the magnificent hills covered in trees
The rippling brooks and the luscious green vales.
With brothers and sisters, I grew up on a farm
Mother was hardworking, Father was stern.
One night I awoke and my tooth it did ache
Pulled boots on, too tight for the journey to make.
Five miles to the dentists alone I did walk
Where creatures like badgers and foxes did stalk.
Up at five in the morning to work on the farm
Then a long walk to school, but it did us no harm.
Back to the ploughing with the help of the shires,
The cows needing milking, by hand, in the byres.
In the fields there were haycocks, no nice tidy bales,
But nowhere else would I live but this *beautiful Wales.*

Joy Davies

WALES

Wales is the land of my darling
The only man in my life
The father of my children
And I'm his loving wife
He reminds me of the mountains
So reliable and strong
And when he speaks, his lilting voice
Is like listening to a song.
A man who is proud to live in Wales
Sings its praises for all he is worth
He loves the mountains, valleys and shores
He thinks it's the best place on earth.

June Davies

WALES

Wales the Land of Legend,
The place where I belong.
Land of true tradition,
Land of stirring song.
Land of many mountains,
Valleys, lakes, and streams
If ever I should leave you
You'd still be in my dreams.
Your legends tell of many things
Of fairy tales of love and kings.
Of brave King Arthur's knights of old
When every knight was brave and bold.
Of towering castles, cottage small,
Of fiery dragons feared by all.
I love to hear these stories told
I'll tell them too when I am old.

Beryl Bright

MAERDY 1968

Hope-groping coal-pit boys
Hew-hacking bent in double
Working in jack-hammer noise
Scrambling down through crow-black rubble
While *they* are full of gliding joys
With wives of cocktail party poise
We'll rise, light-blinking, in grey stubble
Minds packed with hire-purchase trouble
They'll play with their executive toys
And wonder . . . when we burst their bubble.

T D Breverton

THE BLACKNESS OF THE PAST

Bright sunbeams alive with dancing black dust,
Settling on everything, forming a crust.

Dusking the windows and sooting the floors,
Blacking the fingernails, sinking in pores.

Black pats, that scurry to hide in the walls
Will carpet the floor when the deep darkness falls.

Black scum on the river, still and obscene,
Mudding embankments and smothering green.

Coal-dusted Dad, coming home in the morning,
Greets his transient children as they arise yawning.

He washes away his carbon black stink
With black-bubbled soap, in a bath made of zinc.

His sleep is a respite from labour and strife.
Time is a thief stealing light from his life.

Fingermarks blacken the miner's white bread;
And to pit blinded ponies leftovers are fed.

He hears the roof cracking; an ominous sound,
Soon the coalminer is crushed to the ground.

Black bibled minister, funeral solemn,
To the burial ground leads the black-suited column.

For his soul in God's keeping, the sad mourners pray,
Strains of Caersalem are fading away.

The miner is laid in the earth rich and brown,
No winding gear needed to lower him down.

He won't need his lamp, nor his snapbox and jack,
No pits up in Heaven, no coal-face to hack.

As they come to the end of the long mournful hours,
They soften his grave with fluttering flowers.

What price the coal to keep home fires burning
When blood is shed to keep the wheels turning?

God hasten the day when the blackness will pass
And the wounds of the earth will be stitched up with grass.

Megan O'Leary

THE HOMECOMING

That land of Wales where I was born,
Will always be dear to me
My heart will always linger
In that haven across the sea.

Although I am so far away
From the land that I love most,
I see them still, those craggy cliffs,
Along its rugged coast.

The mountains and the valleys
The fields and trees I know,
I'll roam there in the future
As I did so long ago.

And now I am returning
To that beloved land
I feel that I was guided
By God's protecting hand.

The sorrow of the parting
Lies forgotten in the past.
No more sorrow in the future
I'm coming home at last.

Garry Morton-Jones

MINE MISSING

A Welshman I was born,
in the valleys I was bred.
Where the men are big and burly,
and wear lamps upon their head.
Growing up in a mining town,
seeing contented, grubby faces all around.
The chief support of living, extracted
directly from out of the ground.
Pithead whistles, shaft wheels spin,
the dawn is broken by the familiar din.
A tight community, one and all,
when the town is woken by the pithead call.
As memories fade, and eyes grow weak,
familiar sounds are what we seek.
But progress wins to the final score,
Of a mining town being no more.

Michael George

HOME COUNTY

Rambling boots sound the lane
Seeking pastures new again
Rock and crag to ascend
View the hills, the river's bend.
Patchwork fields, dry stone wall
Watch the evening shadows fall,
The meadow holds its black-faced sheep
Graze their way, around the feet
Of Saxon tombstones, crumbling now.
Church and farm and wayside flowers
Stately homes, cathedral boughs.
All and more, can be seen
In Derbyshire, a vale so green

P Hill

HOMELAND

Wales is my homeland the land of song
With gold-coloured daffodils that glisten in the sun
Up in the mountains the castle stands high
With trees that surround it that reach to the sky

We celebrate St David's Day
Springtime is here at last
With juicy currant Welsh cakes
That will soon be in the past

The dusty miner comes home from work
From slaving down the mine
So happy he's lived another day
For he's lucky to still be alive

Wales is the best at rugby
The Dragon makes them proud
With the feathers flying up on top
And the support and a cheer from the crowd

Welsh ladies dance to an old folk's song
Reminding them of old times they knew
The Welsh harp playing a soothing tune
They'll be dancing their hearts out till noon

Brave Gelert was a hero
But his master was misled
And so because of his foolishness
Brave Gelert is now dead

When Mam and Dad are sitting
By the fire which burns Welsh coal
I'm proud I'm Welsh and no one else
I feel Wales deep in my soul.

Kathryn Fenlon (10)

SPEEDWELLS AT LLANTHONY

On a bright day
Restless after winter's hibernation
I was called by sun and skylark's song on high
To wander where the hills rise green.

Sun-drenched, the lanes ran white
And leafing trees stirred sweetly fresh.
From a far field lowing cows and distant shouts
Made sharp sounds on exquisite silence;
And I came to Llanthony.

There stood the ancient, holy pile
Remote, but not yet desolate.
Upon its walls enraptured pilgrims gazed
Seeking a blessed peace.

But I, bewitched, looked long upon a mist
Spreading itself in length on grassy aisle;
Demure, and frequently unseen in hedge and mead,
Here speedwells in profusion bloomed,
Untrampled and revered,
Blue as a cloak abandoned
By the Queen of Heaven.

Hilda M Evans

RIVER OF LIFE

Flowers shake free their gilded golden heads,
they glide to grace heaven's purest source:
to the waters where lust leaves its sorry bed
and joins the many shapes of nature's course.

They drift in time, through the days and years,
and ride the storms (sweet surging swells)
'til they float a slow-slow still in placid mere:
come to rest in green-gladed dewy dell.

For in life we tread no petalled paths -
our lives are mapped by the whims of gods,
No matter now, our beating hearts may laugh,
or cry, they ride the waves that are their lot.

Meirion Owen

CELTICA

Hear glistening blistering barnacled rocks
And the springing sounds of Aberdyfi's bells
See storm-mangled seaweeds and fronds
And stare at the scudding spindrift swells

Bend the clawing trees
And force old leaves to scurry
Romp rampant through a hedge
And cause the sheep to worry

Fox stumble in a gust
Ash humble to the thrust

Crack the crippled branches
Crash waters over stones
Cascade grey white waves
And crush the rock to bones.

Hares fumble in their lust
We grumble about rust

Rooks crawl through the air
Black crows hover like kestrels
Crabs hide in their lair
And fish can hear the bells

Skulls crumble into dust
Crowns crumble from the crust.

T D Breverton

A VISIT TO THE LAKES

One sunny afternoon,
A trip out was planned
To visit the lakes in the green mountains
Of Wales.
So with a picnic packed and children in tow
We set off for a joyous ride
Plenty of scenery for all to see.
Trees and green grass, with plenty of sheep.
Buzzards and kites flying free in the sky.
Plenty of fresh air, with mountains so high.
Then the lakes are soon in view
Just like in the movies, of the blue lagoon
Clear blue waters are seen for miles.
No pollution or smoke could be seen.
Just beautiful clean air.
And lots of green trees.
It all felt like a dream.
You could even think that
Canada had been transported
Over to Wales
As such a wonderful sight could
Be found in the mountains of Wales.

M Jones

WALES

I've always in lived in Wales,
since the day I was born,
it's such a lovely place to be,
in the valleys in the morn.

The yellow of the daffodils,
the green of the leeks,
the red of the Welsh dragon,
the singing in the streets.

The football and the rugby,
the anthem sung out aloud,
the youngest to the eldest,
they stand there very proud.

I cannot speak the language,
I find it hard you see,
but Wales is where my heart is,
it's where I want to be.

Robert L Peters

PLYMOUTH DREAMING

Sailing boats
Whisper through the Sound
Safe and sound.
Steady beats a heart
Beside the sea;
Between Tamar and the Plym,
Plymouth lies dreaming.

Pilgrim Fathers
Mayflower
. . . or may not.
Drake, determined,
. . . to take his time.
At Plymouth Hoe
The sea stops
and waves:
A city nestles, nods and spreads,
Stretches out
Towards the silent moor . . .
. . . and yawns.
This is the place for me.

June Lloyd

ILSON TOWN

Me home is in the Derbyshire hills
Ayup me duck here's lots of thrills
Where'er ya look is mountains sweet
Covered in grass an easy fa feet

We Ilson folk are happy folk
Ayup me duck time fa a joke
In Ilson Town we're all awrate
So come and see us one day mate

Off ta market wi' me kid
Ayup me duck giz a quid
Ya'll meet folks ya know up there
A good day out wi'out a care

Listen mate dunna miss this town
Derbyshire huntin? Track us down
Reckon ya'll want ta come and stay
If ya've bin down Ilson way

M E Kirkman

THE HEBRIDES

In the West
On a green isle
You led
The solitary life

For God was
Around you
Within you
In every movement
And gesture

The stages of redemption
The great mystery
Your small
        Coracle
In the vastness
        of the ocean.

Jules Ronay

THE LEGACY OF A COAL MINER

The pits have gone we knew so well
Black diamond coal the mines did sell
The pithead winding wheel is gone
Its noise is now a distant song
The black-grimed faces, helmets tilted
Daffodils flowered but then they wilted
The pithead baths a distant thought
Like coal dust lessons we were taught
The songs that echoed down the lane
Of sweat and tears, of grief and pain
Mixed with valour, love and joy
Shared by miners man and boy
The price they paid to dig the coal
From deep within that blackened hole
Was it worth the cough-racked lungs?
Legacy of the dust as bells are rung
Another grave beside the mine
Where once the pithead wheel did whine
What is the price that men have paid
As earth's resources we made them raid?
Mates they were there in the dark
Not many left but they have made their mark
No more will we ever suffer in the pit
For at last there is now an end to it.

Vicky Lee

WELSH FLAG

White horses in procession
Waves rhythmically lashing windswept shore
Sombre stillness of mariner's church
Nestled in restful arm of River Tawe and the sea
Bleached stone walls of fisherman's cottage.

Green sharp contoured valleys
Scarred and shadowed, untouched by sunlight
Headlands of velvet viridian grass
Wild flowers a palette of patchwork beauty
Filigree of ivy on ancient castle walls.

Red brick of deserted factory chimney
Reaching skyward from derelict site
Crimson light at sunset dissolving in rippled sea
Horizon consuming its own reflection.

Three majestic colours united
White background, green foreground, emblematic beast
Images of Wales
Symbol of a Nation.

Patti Smith

WATERFALLS ON SKYE

We went over to Skye, with its sunshine and warm winds,
Over to Skye on a beautiful day.
A'sailing we went, on the graceful boat ferry
Peace and tranquillity, bay to bay.

The hills and the heather, the seagulls, the breeze,
Gladdened our hearts, as we wandered there.
Here, we said, was the ultimate beauty,
Which we would remember, for many a year.

Nightfall came softly, and with it the rain,
First it came gently, but now pouring down,
As morning awakened, we gazed from our window,
Never such beauty had wrapped us around.

Waterfalls! Waterfalls! Glittering waterfalls!
Rushing and gushing, who knows where or why.
Just waterfalls, waterfalls, raging and wonderful,
Let it rain, let it pour, all was beauty on Skye.

Margaret Morton

MY HILLS

Longing for my hills of home
So quiet and peaceful where I used to roam
Happy and free on a summer day
Just talking to God in my own special way.

I used to climb those hills up to the top
My feet used to tell me it was time to stop
I wanted to reach the clouds up high
As the sun came through!
                    Pushed them out of the sky.

God made my hills for me to feel free
Like walking in heaven a wonder to see
Birds singing their little song
Life was so right then nothing was wrong.

I still thank God in my prayers today
My tears still fall as I'm far away
But I see my hills as I sit and sigh
In my dreams I will walk them until I die.

Flo Davies

Oberffaith Hedd I Ddagrau Glas - From Perfect Peace To Blue Tears

Drws-y-Coed's open door and rugged face
awashed with love am I for your lost embrace,
Here beautiful mountains meet to tempt and
ease the human soul to never-ending peace,
Down the hill I wander still
the Nantlle lake long mastered nature's will,
Dark thoughts of gloom dare not intrude
this perfect sea of solitude.
As an awakening nightmare I look and stare
they bare the pity of this day
Hills of slate amassed over years
grown from seeds to form Nantlle's tears,
Light the fuses, blast the face, load the trucks
with dark blue slate, hoist the cradle cable braid
transform the green with mining waste,
See temptations running wild all for profit none for life
Lords of wisdom locked in greed
plucked all the flowers and left the weed,
Future people looking on can all but wonder
where all the profit had gone
Tell them if only the quarries could talk
they'd tell a tale of proud Welsh folk
Who scraped a living from the slate
adjusted all to fill their plate.
We may not understand but compassion
tempts my reasoning
for one day soon the quarries will awake
afresh rejoicing.
A park of splendour with all at hand
museum of riches stored magic wand,
A train to pull the trucks once more
and a mansion with marbled floor,
At times long past when Tal-y-Sarn trembled
to pulsating nailed boots clinging

Here once again the bell of truth will hail
each morning's bringing,
And all will say we staked our claim
to the land that was ours to inherit
But I believe the old miners locked on
and grasped my love of merit.

Mansel Jones

SONG OF THE PEAK

Beautiful Derbyshire, our own lovely peak,
No other scenery do I ever seek,
Beautiful hills, and beautiful dales,
Where still we may find the old Roman trails.
There are limestone walls older than time,
And bright copper trees red as wine,
The sheep graze in peace upon the hill
and all is tranquil, all is still.
Lovely old Dovedale with its stepping stones,
Neat little gardens and thatched roofed homes,
Breathless in wonder, I've spent happy hours,
And seen wells being blessed, dressed in all kinds of flowers.
In romantic Matlock, the lovers' delight
They walk hand in hand on warm summer nights.
They look down on the river from Abraham's Heights,
See boats decked out in lanterns and fairy lights.
I've been in Paris and old Amsterdam,
But best of all I love the place where I am,
I've danced all night in a Belgian festival square
But give me dear Derbyshire, my heart is there.

E C Gray

CHANGING SCENERY, CARDIFF

Aye, Llanishen your environmental status once reigned supreme,
O'er wooded boundaries and farmlands green.
Kindred enjoyed many a ramble o'er your country scene.
Your compound of nature held treasures galore,
Flora, fauna, birds, insects, an education for folk to explore.
Summertime kin walked to Cefn Onn Park,
Starting at dawn returning by dark.
Folk admired your prize-winning station as they waited for a train,
Perhaps to Barry Island and back again.
Scouts, Brownies or Girl Guides trekked along lanes or o'er hillsides.
Children loved the thrill of camping, farms and the olde mill,
Paddling, fishing in your streams, climbing swinging from your trees.
Families gathered blackberries, cobnuts on autumn days,
At Christmas, cones, holly, acorns for nativity displays.
Aye, Llanishen a different scene is on your verge,
As the concrete and steel have begun to emerge.

Pam Ismail

WARWICKSHIRE

W arwickshire is blessed with trees
A nd rolling hills and grassy leas
R abbits run and foxes too
W ildlife in plenty and pigeons coo
I n spring the country is so pretty
C ause life is sprouting in the city
K indred spirits blossom and flourish
S ummer arrives the plants do nourish
H ear the birds singing their songs
I n harmony all day long
R ich colours in autumn - then winter's tale
E verything dies - down comes the veil.

Isabel Hurney

A DERBYSHIRE CHURCH

The church tower peeps above the trees
That sway and rustle in the breeze,
And on the mast a flag flies high
Against the backcloth of the sky.
Perched on a hill - a sentinel it stands
Looking out across the lands.
Many are the people who have worshipped there,
And sung sweet hymns of praise, and knelt in prayer.
The church, 'St James', the place, Crosshill,
A village church that carries on its message still.
Close by main thoroughfare, and country lane -
A place where countless feet have trod time and time again.
Right in the heart of England, not all that well known
Save by the Codnor villagers who've made it all their own.

Freda Searson

LAST FAREWELL

Do not gaze at me with that sad look
Because I know of all the care you took,
And the torment you had within
Because we cannot always win;
Set me down somewhere nice to rest,
For I know you've always done your best;
As you sit and stroke my soft brow
It has come the hour to sleep now;
If you should blink and I am gone
It's time to let go while I travel on;
I leave behind my earthly coat,
For I do not need it where I float.
Think of my going with a little sadness
But remember the times we had with gladness.

Pippin

MORFA DYFFRYN

Early morning's
  dew-draped dawning
stems the camper's dreamy tide.
  Softly stirring,
spirits rising,
  sleep's firm knots are eased, untied.

Surging surfward,
  clothes redundant,
close to nature's rhythmic shore.
  Shrill the happy
children's laughter
  climbs above the timeless roar.

Soft the silken
  sand's forgiving,
muted now the vocal tide.
  Soft the touch
of hand on shoulder
Time suspended turns aside.

All too soon
  are bare feet duneward,
breathless, goose-fleshed, tangled hair.
  Rubbed and cuddled
in the sunshine,
  welcome now the picnic fare.

Late, the evening
  shadows lengthen,
by the water, hand in hand.
  Deeper bronzing,
lightly covered,
  wending home along the sand.

Dave Bissitt

DENBIGHSHIRE

I watch a full moon arising
over the Dyserth Hills
Forget the world around me
The dark satanic mills
Then the moon drifts on and on
And gently disappears
So with it drifts your problems
Your cares, despairs, your fears!

Then looking for more wend careful
way through Denbigh Moors
Deep in the hillsides yet not
too far from seaside shores.
So reaching and finding places
that make history
Still so many areas clouded
in much mystery!

Perhaps you've passed through mountains,
perhaps then by a lake
And in some simple way taken
wrong turn by mistake
Just to find certain views
turning out so heavenly
In beloved Welsh countryside
called *County Denbigh!*

You know the world of nature
An awesome lifetime gift,
How often do you find it
To give your life a lift?
Is not this then the beauty
Of this unusual place
To wake up in the morning
Away from life's rat-race!

Ron Forman

SCARRED BY COAL

Rhondda Valley was peacefully calm
Preserving beauty with natural charm.
The valley was wooded, hills were green.
The river had salmon, water was clean.
In seams beneath the valley laid,
An abundance of coal of finest grade.
The black fuel came in great demand,
As Coal Owners moved to search the land.
With shafts sunk and seams won.
Mining in Rhondda had then begun.
The industry developed at tremendous pace,
As communities settled for a mining race.
Houses were terraced in long straight lines,
Built for men who worked in mines.
A miner's large family, and lodgers too,
Shared bedrooms, tin bath, and outside loo.
Fathers, their sons, men of all ages,
Slaved down pits for low wages.
Digging out coal with shovel and pick,
Where air was thin and dust was thick.
Brave men they were to descend that hole,
And risk their lives to bring up coal.
Over a thousand men went heaven-bound,
In fatal accidents underground.
The collieries are gone, shafts are concealed.
Mining is finished in Rhondda's coalfield.
Tips are landscaped, streams are clean.
Our valley once more is looking green.

Ivor John Williams

COFFEE STALL NEAR SULLY

On a fine evening
between days of summer rain,
we came again to Anna's.

Her stall backed the sea,
shielding her from winds
that make no distinction
between seasons.

She stood welcoming,
like a Bedouin in his tent,
her wide smile dispelling
the dimness of the interior
as she poured coffee, hot, sweet,
into generous cups.

Nearby, a wall, honey-coloured, low
spread its inviting width
along the pebbles' edge.
We took our coffee there,

Felt the day's heat cooling
as we watched an undecided sea
swirling and churning
around Sully Island,
while fading light shaded
from soft blue to softer white

and night, moon-shadowed,
sailed silently in from the bay.

Gwenda Owen

LATE AUTUMN AT ELVASTON CASTLE

Sharp autumn breezes toss and tease
The dying leaves and sighing trees;
In shallow fall and winter's deep
Nature withdraws to silent sleep
Beneath brown rustling carpeting
To lie and dream and wait for spring

Cold lake of cloud-reflecting grey
Muddied by soil, rain washed away;
Raindrops that drip like blood from trees,
Damp mists disturb an earlier autumn's ease.
Reverse of spring warmth, the autumn chills
Warn of coming cold that kills

English Garden, cobbled court and farm
Are closed and quiet, secured from harm;
The park, as if by fairy spell
Recedes into its winter shell
Whilst wrapped within its coat of stone
The castle dreams its dreams, serene, alone

Trevor Smith

I DREAMT I WAS IN DENBIGHSHIRE

I dreamt I was in Denbighshire
The vale where I was born -
I dreamt I was walking in pastures green
on a summer's morn.

I dreamt I heard the blackbird sing
as it flew on the wing.
I dreamt I saw the sea green and blue
under a rainbow of every hue.

I dreamt I touched the silver sand
I dreamt I smelt the gorse on every hand
I dreamt I heard the laughter sweet
of Welsh children playing in the street.

I dreamt I was in Denbighshire!

Lee DaCosta-Harewood

PLYMOUTH JOB CENTRE (UB40)

Have you seen them?
Pasty-faced and haggard,
As they struggle into town.
Full of cares and worries,
That will slowly grind them down.
This is the modern Generation,
Thin, half starved and jobless.
They clutch their UB40s
For the man behind the counter,
To prove they are jobless and not lazy SOB.

Have you seen them?
Standing in the line at the Post Office,
Girocheques clutched firmly in their hands.
Their talk is coarse and ugly,
They slowly move forward,
They become a shuffling, noisy band.
OAPs cover their ears and form another line,
There is no communication between the two.

The old have worked all their lives,
The young ones never will,
So it is a pension or a UB40.

P M Batch

A PLACE CALLED HOME

Denbighshire is a place called home.
A country filled with pride.
I moved down here some years ago.
With my husband by my side.

The air is fresh and very clear.
The sun is bright and warm.
The sky is blue with fluffy clouds,
and the atmosphere is calm.

The sea sends waves upon the sand.
To wash the seashells clean.
The hills are always welcoming,
as they look down on grass that's green.

This little spot in North Wales,
is there for all to see.
This land is worth its weight in gold,
and all of it is free.

Joan Sayers

THE MEMORY

The memory was like darkness in me.
It smothered all: silencing the already muted
Ambition of lucidness. Like a vagabond
It smiled with loneliness and spoke -

In dense terse it began - 'Remember me?
Years have passed,' its closeness tightened like a frown,
'But I still breathe, with all your pain, and all your tears . . . '
And as our tear fell . . . light.

D Craig Kendall

DERBYSHIRE

If you should go through Derbyshire
You have a feast in store
Panoramic views and more
To take your breath away.

The hills and dales and stately homes
The moors ablaze with heather,
You cool your feet on stepping-stones
When walking by the river.

The villages of old-world charm
Dry stone walls and valleys deep,
Rocky heights both stark and calm,
And boats upon the waterways.

You may see the blessing of the wells
When they're dressed with leaves and flowers
To show us what the Bible said
In a glorious feast of colour.

But on the skyline you might see
A black and grim reminder
Of the men who toiled below the earth
To bring us coal to warm us.

But adding there to Nature's charms
Are others made to please you
Steam trains, adventure parks and farms
And fun to suit all ages.

Where would you find a place more full
Of beauty and of splendour,
Of people rare and wonderful
Except maybe in heaven.

Emma Hunt

DERBYSHIRE

Set in the peaks of the middle land
The county of Derbyshire does stand,
a county with a rich tapestry,
of villains, martyrs and history.

The mystic circle of Arbor low,
where nine young ladies dared to go
They tempted fate they're all alone,
and ended their days turned to stone.

And if you pass old Eyam's doors
remember events from years before,
the splendid cloth from London Town,
that brought that little village down.

A maiden, Mary, suffered much pain,
Impeding Henry's heir to reign.
Imprisoned in an awesome place,
Wingfield Manor still bears that trace.

From land of Scots through many a town,
A proud parade to steal the crown,
The Bonnie Prince spoiled many plans,
Whence he withdrew his troops from Derby's lands.

The Cromford story plain to see,
Visions of Arkwright's industry,
Housing, employment - a bountiful crop,
A problem the Luddites just could not stop.

The lady with the lamp graced Derbyshire's door,
living at Holloway for five years or more,
her lives dedication gave her the will,
to help the needy and cure the ill.

Derby County - the premiership - the present day,
what really is there left to say?
They prefer to forget parts of their past,
but they are premiership now and it's meant to last.

Alison Doyle-Stevenson

ROBIN RED

O' how I love thee, robin red,
Thy jaunty gait, blithe bob of head;
Thy golden bill, prized treasure rare,
Nought could surpass notes borne of there;
'Midst thicket deep, sweet strains rejoice,
Bring warmth through winter with thy voice,
And make a weary heart more whole,
Thou art the voice that stirs my soul.

Of robin red my heart speaks true,
Thy doublet primed with scarlet hue,
A hint of blush on frosted white,
Heralds spring pigment, warmth and light;
Peruse thy haunt and guard her well,
'Gainst feathered raids, through arctic swell;
With fierce affray defend thy lair,
Such valour, doth my spirit stir.

Sweet robin red thy anthem sing,
Each season lists unto thy ring,
All change is mirrored in thine eyes,
Of stark, black jet, 'neath fickle skies;
O' loyal friend thou dost not flee,
When autumn grips upon each tree,
Thy roots hold fast on nature's vine,
To bless this land and heart of mine.

Sharron Hunt

SEASHORE HERITAGE

Clean, sparkling sand in tranquil bay,
Grey gulls scream, waves toss free;
With laughing faces, children play.
Small dogs prance in the sea,
Bouncing dinghies dance on the tide,
Exulting with colourful pride.

The seashore our finest playground,
Sandcastles, moats and flags;
Shrimping, swimming, surfing spellbound,
Commandos behind crags,
Six thousand miles, Britain's coastline,
Buoyant bathing in pure sunshine.

Over one hundred lighthouses,
Guide ships around our shores.
Eddystone off Plymouth, houses
Pleasant rooms on nine floors.
Southend's long pier stretches one mile,
With shows, snack-bars to rest awhile.

Seaweed, most versatile product.
You can eat it, wear it;
From it, glass, yarn, paper, construct,
Bread, ice-cream and junket.
For health, rich in potassium,
Iodine and magnesium.

The boisterous breeze shore-ward blows,
Wild waves smooth littered sand.
Like ocean depths, endless truth grows,
All strife and wrong withstand.
Compassion flows from shore to shore,
The Eastern Cross shall wane no more.

James Leonard Clough

A VIEW OF HILLS

If you ever visit Devon, you will not need many skills
to realise that this county has an awful lot of hills.
And this may be the reason why so many people love it;
our county's awe-inspiring when you're standing high above it.
My home is halfway down a hill; to leave it I ascend,
and when I reach the hilltop my emotions always tend
to be of awe at all the hills and valleys stretched in front of me,
traversed by ever-changing light and shade, a living tapestry.

Off to the east is Culmstock Beacon high upon the moor,
its presence made apparent by the hut without a door.
This may seem odd, but there's a reason why it should be so:
the local people took the door down many years ago,
because one day a donkey pushed the door and made his way inside,
and then, shut up inside the hut, the poor old donkey died.

Southeast, on clear days, I can almost look out to the sea,
but, shoulders hunched, more hills conspire to keep the view from me.
They tease, these hills; at Sidmouth Gap they dip as if they might,
perhaps, reveal a hint of blueness, but they guard it from my sight.

Much nearer, as the year proceeds, I get to see the tide
expressed in ever-changing colours in the fields on close hillsides.
From brown to green to yellow, then once more to brown or green
the hillside flickers, showing where the crops are now, or where they've
been.

And then, south-westward, all the hills stand hierarchically,
their crests subservient to Dartmoor in its highest majesty.
With regal loftiness the moor may choose not to appear
unless it's shown off to advantage when the weather's bright and clear.

And westward, close at hand, a group of huddled trees declare
that once, shored up by steep-flanked hills, a settlement stood there.
The earthen banks that once gave people somewhere safe to go
have, as the years passed by, been just the place for beech to grow.

Helen Thomas

PERSONAL NEED

With silent sorrow I will meet tomorrow
Just like I greeted today
In a lonely daze trapped in a maze
I will struggle to find my way

Through all the rubble and constant trouble
That life thrusts into view
Through all the mines of forgotten times
With only the memory of you

To keep me pure and soft secure
As I venture to the world alone
Driven not by greed but the personal need
To make your innocent dreams well-known

To the ones who dare to acknowledge they care
About the state of affairs we see
And who'll join the race to make a better place
For now and for infinity

And on that day when the white doves play
I will take my irrelevant life
And find you where the bright eyes stare
And make you my celestial wife

But until that hour I will gather each flower
And lay it by a cemetery gate
Through sun and rain till we meet again
I will know my earthly fate

Simon Vanstone

AN AFFIRMATION

I have the right to live as I choose
To speak as I see fit
To act with my own freedom
To love without guilt.
Within me lies the strength to assert these rights
The voice to speak my thoughts
The courage to plot my own course
And define what love is to me.

I will respect the views of others
But they must respect mine,
I will not be forced to live another's life
For thus does the spirit die.
Having felt the insipid approach of such a death
And having broken free of such
I will exult in my own right to live
And grow in the nurturing arms of my true being.

Rose Stuckey

THOUGHTS OF WORCESTERSHIRE

What does Worcestershire mean to me
Apart from peace and tranquillity?
The place where I spent childhood days
Under pale blue skies and summer haze
Always a view of the Malvern Hills
To cheer the spirit and cure one's ills
Fresh air in the lungs and country smells
The familiar sound of cathedral bells
A lonely tractor ploughing up the land
Friendly faces, the Sally Army band
Playing carols round the Christmas tree
That's what Worcestershire means to me

Charline Shearer

ATTENBOROUGH NATURE RESERVE

The sunlight dazzles on the water here
Where, once, brown cattle grazed the riverside,
When water meadows lay along the wide
And verdant washlands down to Beeston weir.
Then came the gravel-seekers who left drear
Unsightly gaping pits, no trees to hide
The shattered landscape, formerly the pride
Of Attenborough; desolation near
To Church and village. But when nature cares,
Beauty will be restored as in this place
Where now the sunlight plays. Willow and reeds
And sedges grew by bleak lagoons, and pairs
Of moorhens breed. Diving grebes surface,
And man and nature work to serve their needs.

Sheila Town

THE BRIDGE

Love is the bridge which eases the pain
Of death, whether by illness or war,
Accident or old age. Know
That love endures, forms a bridge
Between the worlds, this and the next.
Thoughts may be shared, memories too;
Realise a presence beside you,
Perhaps a familiar perfume.
Weep not, grieve not for yourself;
Rejoice that your loved one is safe,
Free as a bird in a new body of light,
Able to hear all thoughts, kind or not,
Able to love maybe more than before.
Let love be the bridge which eases the pain.

Diana Myers

MY VALENTINE

Valentine please say you will
be mine forever more.
To be with me, through all life's ways
and want me more and more.

I want you as my Valentine
no one else will do.
I want to be your Valentine
and make our dreams come true.

I'll try to make you happy
in everything we do,
together we can go through life
sharing our love so true.

Darling please say you'll be mine
to hold the whole night through,
your love means so much to me
because I love you true.

Deane Hulland

REFLECTIONS ON CHELTENHAM

Is it the same sun that sets on Cheltenham
That bakes dry some foreign locale?
The same warm wind that strokes the trees here
When there's a howling gale?
Or the gentle rain that kisses the earth
Soon washing rude dwellings away?
I cannot think it in this town so fair
On this glorious summer day.

David E Burke

SHORT LIFE

Bright he was, loved life a-plenty.
Then he upped and left at twenty.
'He had not lived,' they said. 'Too young!'
But life it was that quietly sprung.

No crashing end on motored wheels,
No tortured flesh or painful wheals.
Just drowsiness, the final sleep,
The silence made the angels weep.

So sound no muffled bell for him,
Who left our sea in early swim,
But show his corpse, pale, white and still,
To those who would the moment thrill.

They look so simple, pills and cans,
With promise of the joy that spans
The universe of delight and bliss.
But no one sees the coward's kiss.

For life goes to the brave and swift,
Not those who waste the precious gift
By pandering to a doubtful whim,
The promise of a solace slim.

Just two small pills were all it took,
With leering wink and knowing look.
None could tell them, they were clever,
They were going to live forever.

Peter Lacey

BARNSTAPLE FAIR

The train hurtles in, we stop and stare,
at the wondrous sight of Barnstaple Fair,
With all its great attractions, we mingle with the crowd,
Gazing at the carousel, spinning round and round.

      'Shall we go on the bumper cars,?'
      a little boy declares;
      'No,' says his friend,
      'The flying chairs.'

We decide to try the coconut shy,
Big dipper being much too high.
'Roll up, roll up, five balls for a pound,
Try and knock the skittles down.'
'A toffee apple I must try,
Maybe also a hot mince pie'

      'What about the ghost train?'
      'Shall we venture on?'
      'I'm game if you are,'
      'Let's go along.'
Going through the darkness, spiders we feel,
Tickling our necks, 'Glad they're not real'
All good things must come to an end,
'Run out of money,' no more to spend.

      It's been a good day,
      Weather fine,
      I know we'll come
      Again next time.

Wendy Watkin

THE SEASONS

Oh to be in Devon when winter colours form.
Fir cones, sticks and berries amidst a frosty lawn.
Holly and berberis beside the fences grow.
Bitter icy winds through snow decked branches blow.

Oh to be in Devon when springtime colours form.
Dainty little snowdrops amidst a crispy lawn.
Fragrant creamy blossom on sparse green hedges grow.
Icy cool breezes through budded branches blow.

Oh to be in Devon when summer colours form.
Daisy with sweet clover amidst a fresh mown lawn.
Multitudes of berries on stately rowans grow.
Fresh warm breezes through leafy branches blow

Oh to be in Devon when autumn colours form.
Leaves and russet apples amidst a patchy lawn.
Shiny golden ivy on rocky ledges grow.
Chilly wet winds through bare twigged branches blow.

Oh to be in Devon, winter, spring, summer and fall.
Through the seasons of the year.
A special time for one and all.

Linda Mary Hodgson

LADY GODIVA

She was young pious and a beautiful lady.
Fearing and serving God with all her being.
It was in despair to her husband she did appeal
to remit certain impositions from the inhabitants of Coventry

He promised to relieve them from the heavy taxes.
If she would ride naked through the town.
This she agreed to do having just passed the word around.
All blinds and shutters to be drawn then a ransom
                                        she would obtain.

Coventry people are proud of her memory
A statue was erected in centre of town
Upon her faithful white horse she sits
Golden hair a dangling down.
If ever you are in Coventry visit the Lady Godiva
who set her people free.

Irene Barton

THE WAY US IS

'Tis bootiful yer in Debbin,
Some volks says us is maze,
But they'm always yer on holiday,
They stands and watch the cattle graze,
Walking down are country lanes
They spots the local pub,
Us might be maze, but most of all
They likes ar' olsome grub,
Sum zinks a pint of zyder,
The village varmer made,
Then they zounds even dafter,
As they makes their way to bade,
They zeems to think us stands around
Wiv straw between are teef
Fitted out in long white smocks
Wiv nort else underneaf,
They likes to visit all the varms
Feeding this and that,
But wish they had are wellie boots
When they vinds their first cow pat,
There's nowhere quite like Debbin
Us got a lingo of ar' own . . . and
If city volks don't like it
They'd better off at home . . .

Marcia Luxon

MEMORIES OF DEVON

Cider apples on the trees.
Blossoms fluttering in the breeze.
Snowdrops heralding the spring.
Across the fields the church bells ring
Fields that look so fresh and green.
Strawberries and clotted cream.
Dartmoor standing lone and bleak.
Exmoor with its highest peak.
Famous names come to mind.
Grenville Drake and Golden Hind.
Kingsley who wrote 'Westward Ho'
Westward Ho where strong winds blow.
Lorna Doone who never wed.
Never made it - died instead.
Tom Cobley and the old grey mare
Going on to Widecombe Fair.
Of all the counties in the west
Glorious Devon is the best.

Anne Purves

BRUM

Yes! I'm a Brummie and proud of it too.
We're always put down 'cos we say Yo instead of You.
Our hearts are as big, if not bigger than most,
Yet we seem to be laughed at from coast to coast.

During the war we were sisters and brothers -
Always ready to give aid to others.
Our men went to fight - giving their lives,
Leaving their kids and hard working wives.

I remember the days of the trams and the horses pulling carts.
The days of unemployment, empty plates and broken hearts.
I've lived for almost eighty years -
I've heard the laughter and seen the tears.

Birmingham's changed beyond recognition
Gone are the days when we made ammunition.
Some changes are good and some are bad
But I'll always be grateful for what we once had.

Irene Kelsey

GRAND TOUR

Meriden lies at England's heart,
seems the best place to make a start,
Atherstone home of the milliner,
hats abound for him or her

Nuneaton rich in mineral ore,
Mines and quarries to the fore,
Bedworth has more pubs than most,
just the place to drink a toast

Rugby with its famous station,
providing cement to the nation,
Leamington once with its Royal spa,
makes brakes and clutches for your car

Stratford home of Will Shakespeare,
you cannot move for tourists here,
Henley no this one's in Arden,
Oh no boats! I beg your pardon,

The castle high in Warwick stands,
the county town surveys its lands,
seems a fitting place I'm sure,
to bring an end to our grand tour.

Robert Young

THE ROYAL FOREST OF DEAN

I love my visits to the Forest of Dean
- slate and grey-stone abodes shoe-horned in,
there's something about this higgledy-huddledum,
this chaos of weather-sculpted stone,
smooth as salt-licks among the uncurling bracken frond.
These Foresters, oldest of English breed
- older than Claudius, King Offa, and the Venerable Bede;
Plots of character, commoners right and deed:
The woolly 'ships' that pant on the curbstone
- by Drybrook via Stenders, by Gorsty Knoll, and Blaisdon.
Foresters are freeminers since 'tyme out of minde',
with 'maddocks' picked at ingots mined.
See the 'hyups' at the margin of High Beeches,
smooth green mound at the midnight maw that inward reaches,
insects now dance
            like dots of fire aflame on gauzy wing,
where sunlight slants
            a glass-gold world by the old brick kiln.
The dereliction oft bleak but ne'er downcast;
rusted shack, overgrown truck, tumble-down and pebbledash.
To this day old Hugh on the road to Speech House,
talks to the driver of 'the reg'lar double-decker buzz!'
they talk of purple splendour, or thundery weather,
or 5lb chubb, or Coleford Cricket Club;
then he might say, 'O say yew, I'll serve 'ee a drop o'fuel,
just as soon as oi hev finished waterin' my mini Lyn Bartholomew!'

Geoff Taylor

A Day In Oxford

Going out, for an exciting day,
To Oxford city, on the train,
Waiting on platform, in the bay,
It's twenty minutes late, again,
The train comes rattling, to a halt,
Into the carriages, and off with a jolt,
Passing, through the countryside,
Under small bridges, and narrow bends,
To Oxford City, known worldwide,
Under-graduates, and modern trend.

Churches, colleges, and quaint buildings,
Hustle and bustle, of noisy crowds,
Sight-seeing, and window shopping,
And traffic sounding, very loud,
Walking through, college gardens,
Beautiful flowers, in all their fragrance,
Colours of blue, red, and golden,
Strolling on, in peace and silence.

Through the meadow, to the riverside
Watching boats, moving slowly by.
House-boats, brightly painted, in reside,
Ducks and moor-hens, quivering by,
Giving a dip, and dart, in the water,
Anglers, sitting, at leisure, nearby,
Little grey squirrels, on branches high,
What a lovely day, of leisure,
A day of happiness, and pleasure.

Barbara Smith

OUR COUNTY

There's rolling hills and valleys
And rivers wide and free
With hedges blooming sweet with flowers
That's Oxfordshire to me
There's country lanes and woodlands
And quaint old village greens
With rows of country cottages
That's where I want to be
There's stately English buildings
With towering spires to see
And bustling city centres
For shopping, fancy free.
So come and see our county
The pride of all who dwell
And as you leave and go away
You know that all is well.

Sheila Elkins

WARWICK CASTLE

Whenever I go to Warwick town
I must visit the castle too
And as I stand beneath its walls
To admire the lovely view
I try to picture in my mind's eye
The medieval times of days gone by
I conjure up the pretty scenes
of ladies fair - king and queens
Banquets - jousts and knights so bold
These walls have watched them all unfold
And even to the present day
Tourists flock from miles away
For Warwick Castle's history
Is full of life and pageantry.

Joan Jones

WARWICKSHIRE

In the midst of our pleasant country,
A shire of beauty stands.
We love our leafy Warwickshire,
With its gently rolling lands.

So many pleasant lanes to roam,
So much to see and do,
The lovely fields so rich and green,
A sight for me and you.

Our many little villages,
So neat and picturesque,
Create a peaceful atmosphere,
That everyone respects.

Another thing that's interesting,
Its history of long ago,
Our Warwick Castle standing proud
So much to see and show.

Then Kenilworth Castle also,
Its ruins to explore,
Just takes one back to long ago,
To days and years of yore.

Then, too, our famous Stratford,
Which is known so far and wide,
The birthplace of our famous bard,
Who there did once abide.

We love our Midland countryside,
So far from waves and sea,
And we know there is no other place,
Where we would rather be.

A E Kendall

LEAFY COUNTY

Was there ever such leafy grandeur
  To be found the country wide
As here in England's centre
  The wonders of nature's pride -
Represented by the willow -
  Lime and elm and elder as
Where the oak and ash abide
  Great of girth and height
In large numbers grow
  Each species side by side,
Combining thus to create
  A vista of delight
Knowing not of man's divide
  Or hatred of each other
Stand together firm and stout
  As tho' each were a brother.
Heads proudly held aloft
  Gently bowing with the breeze
In unison this way and that
  Whilst birds fly in and out
Requiring only shelter if-you-please
  To spread their simple kind about
Ever free and safe in the arms of trees.

J R Eading

PENN COMMON

Vapour starts welling from the vale
In four o'clock's sudden chill.
The copse riddles with muttering crows.
Horses clatter at the gate.

A broken low wall
By the stump of the Saxon cross
Hides the leaf-closing herbs,
Belying the rising degrees.

The wooded path is drying,
Shoots break through the turf.
Shadows swing in slow season arcs
In the protractor of the eve.

Andrew Strange

WALSALL ILLUMINATIONS

Go to the Walsall lights
In the beautiful arboretum
Cascades of colour, on autumn nights
I tell you, you can't beat 'um
People come from everywhere.
By train, coach and car.
Partake of this annual affair
They are the best in the land, by far.
They've been going now, for over forty years
Each year they have got better.
You'll not be disappointed, have no fears.

Walsall is famous for lots of things
Like Sister Dora, leather, and J K Jerome
But the pleasure, that the lights bring
You'll remember, treasure, and take home.
In your memory, they will stay
Of this you can be sure.
Lights on lovely autumn nights, won't go away
They are a permanent lure.
To come to Walsall lights, it must be, a must.
To stroll around the park with lights aglow.
Every night for a month, after dusk.
It's a trip of a lifetime. Just go.

N Stokes

WARWICKSHIRE - MY HOME

Leafy Warwickshire has always been known
for the peace and tranquillity of the countryside around.
Warwick itself is a busy market town
With its half timbered buildings, the name is renowned.

A castle that sits like a lady on a lake
the view from the bridge is no less than great;
And yet she gives the awe of serenity
And when lit at night just reeks of longevity.

Jousting knights on horseback are taunted
A tower that is supposedly haunted
Don't ye be afraid - ye just be bold
Warwickshire is great for both young and old.

Whether in the north, south, east or west
Everyone can find something they like best
Even a joker if you fancy a jest
Warwickshire stands up to, and plays in, the 'test'.

Throughout the whole of this magnificent shire
There are places to visit - knowledge to acquire
From country parks with boats for hire
To our Collegiate Church with a superb choir

Such wonderful amenities in Warwickshire abound
Still places to go where there's not a sound.
Whether a picnic or a bit of bird spotting
Warwickshire has everything - even designer shopping.

So whatever the mood - if I feel like a roam
Or stay and watch squirrels in the garden - not gnomes!
'Nothing to do' is never my moan
Living in Warwickshire, this place I'm proud to call home.

Margaret Clarke

BRUM

Oh Birmingham city centre
That great concrete sarcophagus
Your streets are lined
With the memories of my youth
A Brummie born and bred
I remember the 70s and early 80s particularly well
Night-clubbing at the Rum Runner
Talking to Duran Duran
Before that the atrocities of the IRA
A city bought to its knees by two bombs
The needless pain and deaths.
Oh Birmingham, we Brummies still love you
Carry on Brum
The Bullring still smiles on you
The Rotunda still there
Pedestrianisation has helped calm the scene
The Evening Mail, seller, his stall remains
The two big opposing soccer teams
Oh Birmingham, Brummies and alike salute you
Into the next century and beyond.

Paul Stokes

WARWICKSHIRE

Warwickshire.
From the fosseway,
to the ridgeway,
to see Warwick on a clear day.
From Edgehill,
to Wattling Street,
the counties people all meet
beneath,
the bear and ragged staff.

Roy Storey

WARWICKSHIRE, MY HOME

The castle at Warwick is one of
the gems in the Midlands' crown.
There are hamlets and villages and
tiny pubs ranging from country to town.

Stratford boasts being the birthplace
of the greatest writer the world has known.
The Americans visit, and they would like
to take it back, and call it their own.

Kenilworth is a market town with
Tudor cottages for all to see.
How nice to travel around Leamington Spa
and call into Barford for tea.

Mighty Coventry is in Warwickshire
Not West Midlands as it is now called.
The Historical fact about this proud city,
is that it used to be walled.

The Germans destroyed the city
under the rubble the spirit remained.
The people of Coventry summoned
their strength, on their city the bombs had rained.

Now there is peace and harmony
in a multi-racial scene.
This wonderful county of Warwickshire
which in summer is bathed in green.

How lucky we are to live here
Free from oppression and strife.
Where we are free to live, and
raise a family and have a contented life.

Kenneth G Roberts

WARWICKSHIRE'S PAST

Land of leafy Warwickshire, such past treasures you behold.
Your enchanting Forest of Arden, Warwickshire's woodland of old.

In your ever-changing landscape like echoes from the past,
remains of buildings and earthworks form a fitting epitaph.

To that of the ribbon weaver daily at the loom, sitting many
hours a day in a cold and stark bare room.

To the toils of labourers in the fields and those of stone
and coal.

To the trials, the hardships and glories of life that now
remain untold.

Land of leafy Warwickshire you have a chequered past, one of
which I'm proud and feel will forever last.

Wendy A Cooper

BIRMINGHAM

Grey, red and blue,
Tall and medium,
Low squares, oblongs and flats.
An endless stream of traffic.
A perspective line of cars, buses and lorries,
- cream, green, maroon, grey-blue and council yellow.
volumes of black smoke as the bus pulls up,
- continuous noise.
The green-red of Fuji film against the grey sky,
Move-stop-push-jar,
kids getting out of father's car.
Pigeons looking bigger than aeroplanes as they flutter
- in flight
- overhead with their heavy, bulbous bodies.

Sandra Burfoot

SOLIHULL HAS A HEART

A quick browse through my local rag,
Was enough to get me going,
To see the headlines big and bold,
Of a Borough whose compassion is growing.

'Help Make a Child Happy at Christmas',
Is a story that springs to mind,
Silhillians will make a real effort,
To ensure help is given you'll find.

'Concert Cash Help' and 'Grand Auction',
To raise money and convey support,
By helping a Leprosy Mission,
Or a Hospice where funds may be short.

But headlines that strike a real chord,
Such as 'Bosnian Children's Appeal',
Suggest that our little community,
Can give help which is heartfelt and real.

A 'Charity Tee-Off' for cancer,
For children - too ill to cope,
Silhillians will golf for as long as it takes,
If it means just a small ray of hope.

These headlines from one week's edition,
It's obvious for others to see,
To live in a place which is caring and giving,
Where else would I rather be?

Solihull is not just a pretty face,
With affluence to hide behind,
Much deeper, there lives a community,
A more gracious one you will not find.

Vanessa Campbell-Kelly

SOLIHULL TOWN

This town of mine is one of a breed,
It has all a person could need.

When you're born a hospital you yearn,
As you get older a school to learn.

A library for more knowledge,
Then move on to a college.

Each day you could visit the assortment of shops,
You can get anything from a hair cut to frocks.

Then as for food to eat in or take away,
You can get something at most times of the day.

Visit a pub for a drink or three,
But be careful there is a police station you see.

Dance the night away in a club,
Meet someone here for a kiss or a hug.

And if they steal your heart away,
There is even a church for your wedding day.

A fire station a courthouse in case things don't go right,
I'm sure you will not need them but then again you might.

There are things not mentioned because the list is too long,
Like bakers, butchers, and buskers to sing you a song.

So I've praised my town till this page is full,
Now try for yourself my town called Solihull.

M L Hewitt

THE 'LIGHTS'

They keep arriving from far and wide
by coach, car and 'park and ride'.
With accents a plenty they proceed to describe
their painful progress - Walsall's lost tribe.

For yellow brick road read grey tarmac path -
For Dorothy and Toto read all mums and tots -
For real unsung heroes read all Council staff -
How many to change a lightbulb? - Lots and lots and lots!

A tantalising peek can be gained from the queue,
then the 'hallucinations' come into full view.
Sparkling lights reflect in spellbound faces,
Noggin tells them his story - they move on a few paces.

The arboretum shuffle continues - many check for rain,
strangers composing a human train.
Burgers and candyfloss perfume the sky,
whilst the ducks just sit and watch people drift by.

King Kong guards the hospitality tent -
a place no one's been and no one's sent.
A last chance for food - a souvenir or two,
a push, a shove, a trip to the loo!

Every need is cared for - by people who've been there before,
St John's tend the body, the Police the law.
A few 'quid' has bought dream-world to your door,
Tell others what you did - what you saw!

For a precious six weeks
experience a treat,
only one condition -
reality's left in Lichfield Street.

Kevin Steward

REFLECTIONS OF A BYGONE AGE

Cottages stand beside houses of a more recent age,
A reminder of days past before history turned the page.
Woodland and farmsteads to progress they did yield;
Roads in place of countryside, buildings built on fields.

Somewhere not far away, a haven lies behind the scenes,
A sanctuary unravaged by man's destructive machines.
A mill pond afore, abounds with ducks and geese,
where once stood a windmill, sails turned in the breeze.

Behind this pond lies an expanse of rough ground,
where a vast array of nature is there to be found,
A hilly track leads to the calm, peaceful waterway,
along which an aqueduct can be seen not too far away.

Once horse-drawn barges would here tote their wares,
to Birmingham or Stratford, perhaps to a fayre.
Yonder stood a priory, where nuns knelt in prayer,
or walked by the water's edge, to meditate there.

About a mile along the towpath there lies an Inn,
Generations have drunk there, with friends or their kin,
The years have changed its appearance, the location's the same;
it stands by the 'drawbridge' from whence came its name.

Lock keepers and horse-drawn carts no more to be seen;
Making way for the motor car on roads once the lanes had been.
A glance at the road names gives an historical clue,
Windmill, Priory, Aqueduct remain, but alas gone is the view.

Margaret Copeland

CHANGING TIMES

Do you remember a time, in Shirley,
Do you remember a time?
When it wasn't awash with great ribbons of shops,
Just a church and three pubs, a mere countryside stop.
Stratford Road - just a solitary line.

To my first school I walked back in 'fifty-four,
As I clutched my sister's hand.
Up the black ashy path, by Saint James' Church,
To worn classroom desks, all scratched and smirched,
And we played on the billowing land.

In my Shirley file an ordnance map,
Dated nineteen hundred and five
Shows post office, and smithy owned by Wainwright,
Church House, where the Baxters lived, just to the right -
Georgina once taught, to survive.

Near today's Shirley Park stood Shirley Lodge -
Doctor Kneale's house and surgery.
He travelled around in a brougham and horse
With top hat, frock coat and a black case, of course.
And his coachman, John Payne, you would see.

But I can remember a time so clearly,
I can remember a time,
Of bicycle rides, the fresh wind in my face.
Like Edith Holden in Knowle and Packwood, what a place.
Her poems and sketches so fine.

My Solihull Grammar School, Malvern Hall
is owned by Saint Martin's today.
Fatty Arbuckle's, Hemmingway's, Bistros and din
Have taken the place of the Olde Worlde Inn
Guess the microchip's right here to stay!

Shirley Thompson

MEN OF IRON

Did you ever hear the clatter of the steelworks in the night,
Or watch the fiery furnace with its fiercesome glowing light,
Did you ever see a workman with his brow-sweat shining bright,
And his muscles flexed and ready as he strains with all his might.

Have you ever seen a stoker with his shovel in his hand,
Working to a rhythm as though it was his last great stand,
Have you seen him pause to wipe his brow and leave a blackened band,
And have you seen a man so tired that he could hardly stand.

Do you know what he might think of as he feeds the fiery glow,
Perhaps he sees the beauty of a flame-starred magic show,
Do you know if he sees far off lands where sun-kissed breezes blow,
Or a country unpolluted where dust-free flowers grow.

Have you ever worked and sweated till your mottled veins stood proud,
Or even shouted mutely when machines were deafening loud,
Have you ever had the thought that molten steel might be your shroud,
And said a little private prayer with head devoutly bowed.

Can you imagine how it must feel when nerve is put to test,
As a scorching red hot ingot moves towards a heaving chest,
Can you imagine the dedication, the loyalty, the zest,
When a Black Country workman is giving of his best.

Can you stand beside a man of toil and dare to think the worst,
As raising up his brown aled glass he gulps to slake his thirst,
Can you stand to see him down his fourth as though it were his first,
And wonder how he holds it when a lesser man would burst.

Have you stood and admired a working man's broad girth,
Then seen within the constancy and courage, wit and mirth,
Have you stood and acknowledged that by the nature of his birth,
A true Black countryman is the salt of this fair earth.

Olive Hyett

THE B'HAM ONION FAIR

Great excitement, once a year
It was huge, it was exciting
Everyone, rushed to be there
The lights, the music, the rides
Big wheel, up to the skies
Toffee apples, on a stick
Balloons, candyfloss, hats, with 'kiss me quick'
The organ grinder, and his monkey
Hot chestnuts, in a bag
coconuts, try your luck!
Frightening, thrilling rides to be had
Try your strength, and ring the bell
ghost train, bumper cars, crowds
Young and old, all the fun of the fair
Just sixpence, a strip of tickets
Might be, your lucky night
the town you've got, hits the light
Grand prize, big jolly Robert doll
Pink and white, with celluloid face
She's great, just what, the little girl wanted
Or a set of saucepans, for the wife
Perhaps the tea-set in the middle
Try your luck, darts, or rifle range
Sorry sir, better luck next time, what a fiddle!
In dark, post and pre-war days, the onion fair
Made our days, a whole lot brighter
What joy, what fun, to take a child, to that fair in Brum
For one night, it was pure delight.
A few pence, would last all night
Then home we'd go, to dream of all the lights.

Irene G Corbett

YEARS GONE BY

We close our eyes
And our mind displays,
Those bygone years
Of our childhood days,
Skates and spinning tops
Marbles too
Were the toys that we played with
Brought with love from you,

We played with old buttons
Flirting them far,
Trying to win
so we fill up our jar,
Hopscotch and conkers,
Just small silly games
With a lace and a pebble
And small funny names,

We didn't have toys
Like they have today,
But we were all very happy
When we went out to play.

A Kent

A NIGHT AT THE ILLUMINATIONS

Illuminations are a lot of fun,
I eat a big fat 'currant' bun
I see a lot of funny things,
Even birds with coloured wings.

I like the rides with flashing lights,
Also the brightness of the nights.
I see colours blue, red, yellow, green,
I love the big beautiful scene.

Samantha Gill (9)

MY TOWN

I met a man from Birmingham
He asked me where I live
When I said that I live in Dudley
He had advice to give
He told me that my town is dead
That I should move away
To the brighter lights of Birmingham
Where life is free and gay
He spoke of four lane highways
Of modern motorways
Of towering concrete office blocks
Where people spend their days
Come to Birmingham he said
Start your life anew
Dudley has no future
This place is not for you
So I took a train to Birmingham
To search for power and gold
For happiness, contentment
Where my future would unfold
I saw the concrete office blocks
And the modern motorways
Then I thought of Dudley Castle
And the high street market days
I thought of all the Dudley folk
And their caring loving ways
Then I took the train back home again
To stay for all my days.

G A Palmer

194

WALSALL PRIDE

Though I wander far and wide
Always I hear across the miles the homeward calls
To be back in the Black Countryside
To be amid the bustling noisy market stalls

To see the hill top church spire
The beautiful Arboretum, lakes and flowers
The majesty of tall trees to admire
A tranquil town corner for those precious leisure hours

To remember the blue trolley buses of yesterday
The past glories of Sister Dora
Jerome K Jerome he too passed this way
The limestone cavern miners of a time much poorer

Still the leather saddle trade by the world renowned
I see the Saddler's red and white football stadium
So many cosmopolitan rich cultures now abound
A bright new transformed town centre for the Millennium

I see the Bridge clock, still slow! But fresh of face
That concrete hippo still smiling
The Town Hall and Library still so full of old world grace
The illuminations, arcades and malls all so beguiling

Many new images and skylines but the townsfolk never change
I hear their rich and humorous dialect call
As around the world I range
I return to my heritage, I stand tall, full of pride in
this my town Walsall.

Glenys Simner

OUR CANALS

As I walk towards the canal,
I wonder why I'm going that way,
Why not carry on along the main road?
Instead, I tread on the soft soil down to the towpath,
and straight away I feel the refreshing tonic,
away from the populated road,
There is a comfortable peacefulness, close to silence,
With only the faint hum of distant humans and their traffic,
A man-made, yet natural, unspoilt wilderness.

I walk along the water's edge,
Past the wild plum trees, and overgrown blackberry bushes,
I notice playful grey squirrels in the trees,
and little plump ducks swimming gracefully have my attention,
then with sudden movement a fat rat runs over to
the water of glimmering uncertainty
and dives into the dark unknown towards its secret burrows.
That water, deep ongoing, full of dark alluring mystery,
the plants and fish and minibeasts, almost free,
only limited by unfortunate objects of human debris.

The animals, water, wildlife and woodlands merge,
This changing, yet historical, disorderly beauty,
running relentlessly on through industry and smog,
I reach the ornamental old iron bridge,
My footsteps echoing the hooves of the past,
I leave this special place,
The real character of the Midlands,
I know why I like walking that way.

Melissa Perry

UNTITLED

What was untarnished
Is not so anymore
A modern day paradise
Happens in place of what
Could've been Eden
Go to the highest place
Look out, and what you'll see is this
Black and grey, a bleakness
Not just smog in the sky
Instead of eternal beauty
All monsters that stand tall
In a formation of buildings
Hard outer shells . . . no feelings within
Where are the fields . . . full of life
Only left a few a handful at most
Subjected to a parasite, must have been
Consumed by progression . . . money
Lost forever, long after we cease to exist
Life may breed in cities . . . but they thrive in
The home of mother nature more easily
On a moonlit night . . . see but half the stars
Along a busy road . . . you'll see litter
Does anyone really heed recycling
Drive down a lane, with luck
You may see more than infrequent weeds
A flower . . . two or a handful in bloom
What was may not have been better
This country of ours could've been
Somewhat more elemental.

Nasima J Ali

THE BLACK COUNTRY SEAM

Local history tells, of limestone caverns as deep as wells
Of coal and iron ore, the thirty foot seam
Of the birth of industry, and the age of steam
And the development of towns by a river or stream

From a community that survived by working the land
To the honing of craftsmen and the skills of the hand
the birth of the car and the manufacturer's heart
All of these the right conditions did start.

Perhaps in retrospect it's not good being the first
As so many people have now felt the hurt
Of the slump and decline, and all that was bought with it
As the dole cheque replaced the hammer, nail, and rivet

But in isolated pockets where the manufacturing wheels stood still
These people of iron have reinforced their will
And rebuilt the industry, on a small scale at first
Such is the resolve of these people of work

So once again in the future, and the present the task
Is to keep the Black Country as it was in the past
From a community who developed the skills of the hand
The Black Country as a monument to industry still stands.

Chris Davies

CANNOCK CHASE

I gaze in awe at the beauty I see
Displayed before me, and in ecstasy
I ramble on, as if in a dream
Down to the clear and crystal stream.

Down through the valley, over the hill
The sweet scented pines stand so still
And majestic, their branches high,
They seem to almost reach the sky.

The silver birch in her satin gown
The weeping willow whose boughs hang down
Caressing the stream in sheer delight;
The elm, the beech, and the larch so bright.

The deer that gaze with watchful eye,
Are left to roam beneath the sky
In freedom from man's destructive hand
Oh Cannock Chase, in England.

Doreen Mudd

HALLOWE'EN IN DERRY

Thousands pack the Guildhall Square, smiling faces
everywhere.
After many years of toil, fireworks now light up
Lough Foyle.
The city that has seen much pain has now
begun to smile again.
Fathers, mothers, daughters, sons. Whole families
can now, have fun.
Hallowe'en has come to town and is bringing
the barriers down.
There goes the Pope and JFK holding hands
with Ian Paisley, there's Madonna and Father Ted,
Kissing, and their faces aren't even red.
Just below Derry's walls people queue at
the burger stalls, ice-cream vans selling
in October and the Bishop doesn't look too sober.
Painted faces, coloured hair, Gary Glitter,
Yogi bear, get your sparklers, four for a pound
echoes all around the crowd.
It's now a city at ease, in this lovely autumn breeze.
The Martegra could not compare with
Hallowe'en in the Guildhall Square.

John Gallagher

DOWN THE BAGGIES

I've been down the Baggies for many years
I've reached the highs of some good wins
Witnessed the jeers and cheers
And plummeted to depths of defeat for my sins

As standing amongst the passionate hordes
Is a test on the vocal power.
Trying to aspire to the tuneful chords
Is tough when high hopes turn sour.

But I still go along and sing my song
This is my church but I pray
Like a congregation in a Sunday throng
That heaven will be here someday.

There's unity on a crowded terrace
It's an ingredient that's lacking in life
These passionate feelings I dearly cherish
In a world where work means strife.

It's an escape where who knows what
Will happen as the minutes go by.
But the theatre of unexpected forgot
To say be prepared to sigh.

It's only about watching a game with a ball
And cheering on your team
But life is a game where we frequently fall
From grace or to earth it may seem.

Rob Wilkinson

YOU DRIVE ME MAD

You drive me mad at times,
Standing still.
What does it take to get you going?
I thought, it was silly really,
That you would help me go places,
I know, I've probably caught you at a bad time
With a lot going on
But that's no excuse.
Sunday morning's best for you, you've made it clear
But it's not best for me -
I like a lie in.
Where are your priorities?
You seem to favour others most of the time.
I'll stay away, you know.
I say that every day
But this time, I'm warning you
If you don't get a move on,
I'm leaving,
The next chance I have.
Goodbye M6!

Chris Cooper

CANNOCK

The silence of the mine, the silence of the wheel
a town with scars from the past, is now on the heal
a wisdom from fear and filth, enriched with grit and salt
treasured memories never fade, locked in the mind's vault
from a saddened past, a brighter future is on the rise
and this little town of sadness, now has joy in its eyes
time is like a pendulum, both swinging to and fro
this little town of Cannock, where public spirits grow.

T Allbright

PITS OF THE PAST

Reclaimed spoil heaps
Draped in green
Redundant miners
Faces clean
Man-made pools.
And leafy glades,
All green too
In many shades.
The dust has gone
There's noise no more
No belching stacks
As in years before
But ne'er forget our heritage
Ill health, the dust
The meagre wage
When danger threatened
Life and limb
When life below
Was dark and grim
Now as you bask
In peace sublime
Let thoughts wander
Back in time
But not too long,
That life has gone
soak up the sun
Then wander on . . .

Kernel

ME!

I'm the exception to the rule I think.
The 18 year old who doesn't want to drink.
The straw that broke the camel's back.
The train that always goes off track.

I'm the 40 year old that doesn't want to get married.
The one year old who doesn't like to be carried.
The fashion designer with no sense of style.
The marathon runner who can't run a mile.

I'm the bird that can't fly.
The penguin who'll give it a try.
The poet that can't rhyme.
The watch maker who can't tell time.

I'm what's left of Hobson's choice.
The award winning singer who has no voice.
The butcher who's a vegetarian.
The incredible loud librarian.

I'm the English teacher who can't spell.
The salesman who doesn't want to sell.
The chat show host who doesn't want to talk.
The rambler who doesn't like to walk.

I'm different to everyone because I'm me,
Losing that would be my disability.

Katrina Austin

STAFFORDSHIRE CENTURY

Once working man could not read
He ploughed the field and sowed the seed
He sat beside his fire bright
And went to bed and slept at night

Then came the days of mining pits
And working man must use his wits
For there was money to be made
And with his rural peace he paid

In holes near hell the poor man slaved
To make the life the rich man craved
This was the age of the machine
And blackened was the country scene

Then came wars fear and strife
To break our hearts and blight our life
The clouds of war began to fade
A land for heroes then was made

We never had it half so good
And so worked hard the way we should
Until we reached the age of leisure
And all things made to give us pleasure

Now working man is much cuter
He's reached the age of the computer.
They've closed the pits and foundry too
To give us back our tranquil view

Man doesn't plough nor sow the seed
The working man now can read
He doesn't sleep so sound at night
The knowledge apple he did bite.

D Grice

THE CHASE AREA

Wherever you go, friendly people you'll meet
Who turn to you and chat in the street.
They don't know your name, or what you do
They're just so friendly, they speak to you.
Cannock's facelift has improved our town
With baskets of flowers all around.
We have a great theatre with excellent shows
Good amateur groups and people well known.

But climb in a car and drive to 'The Chase'
You can walk for miles all over the place
Perfect for artists and walkers with dogs
Botanists, mushroom and fungi bods.
The German cemetery is the place to visit
To reflect on life and how we live it!
If you're perfectly quiet and have some luck
You may catch sight of a deer - or a buck!

Perhaps you could head towards 'Chasewater'
To see swans and birds in every quarter.
Or go-karts, water skiing and yachts
Power boats, swings - and even a shop!
Try excellent walks if you're energetic
(There's even a train if you want to get it!)
So visit our area if you've no place to go
There's plenty to do - you'll enjoy it, I know.

Patricia Holmes

CANNOCK CHASE

No matter what the season
The trees are always there
In coats of different colours
Or even standing bare
They line the road, reach to the skies
Beauty for all before our eyes

Cannock Chase will live forever
We shall guard it with much care
It's a home for many animals
Who all live together there
Huddled in holes, clamber up trees
Quietly wander, always at ease

The flowers that daily blossom
The fungus too that grows
All have their own sweet beauty
As nature clearly shows
Petals so bright, lasting so long
Some of them fragile, others so strong

Our children too will wonder
How long the trees were there
It's part of our own history
A treasure for us to share
Take a look, it's ours to see
Free and alive it will always be.

Janet Keogh

PRIDE OF STAFFORDSHIRE

Staffordshire county
Is one of bounty,
Both city and town
Show signs of renown.

Lichfield Cathedral
Is known to be small,
But treasures untold
There proudly unfold.

Potteries' china,
None is found finer,
Spode, Doulton, Wedgwood
Especially good.

Shugborough Mansion
Has had expansion,
Museum, farm and hall
Now open to all.

Nearby Cannock Chase
Is a magic place,
With hares, rabbits, birds,
Deer grazing in herds.

Alton Towers Leisure,
Gives purest pleasure,
Switch-backing thrills,
And water flume spills.

Stafford has law courts,
Indoor centre sports,
Hospital, showground,
Precincts to stroll around.

Doris E Briggs

STAFFORDSHIRE

O' Staffordshire my county,
    where Normans did once hail.
The cathedral city of Lichfield,
    known as 'the Ladies of the Vale.'

The dominating forest,
    of outstanding natural beauty.
Once provided noblemen,
    with sport and hidden booty.

For upon Cannock Chase,
    it is fallow deer that roam.
The red squirrel is still believed,
    to have this place as home.

But oh, to mention Shugborough,
    with Lord Lichfield in the making.
The Staffordshire county museum,
    extensive parklands for the taking.

And as for ales and beers,
    Burton, home of brew.
The famous old Bass brewery,
    and Bass shire horse teams too.

Following the river,
    through to Stoke-on-Trent.
The view of all the potteries,
    designs are heaven sent.

O' Staffordshire my county,
    once a passage for the mining.
Is now, but a ghost town,
    once a silver lining.

Bridget George

MY TOWN

I live in the Derry city
On the west bank, of the Foyle,
A lot of history dwells therein.
And it's often 'on the boil'
'On the twelfth of August, every year,
The orange men, they march.
Around! Around! The mulberry bush
And underneath the arch!
On Hallowe'en the best is seen.
And kiddies, all dressed up.
With faces painted, and not so sainted
They eat their apples and nuts!
In World War two! The city grew.
And the Navy, came to stay.
The North Atlantic, to patrol.
And the submarines at bay!
The pubs were stacked
And the dance halls packed
While the sailors danced away
With lovely girls, in high heel shoes,
And figures to 'please the eye'
But that all changed in '69
When the cause was civil rights!
The marching stopped and the guns came out!
And our town was set alight!
But al that's gone, and peace has come
And the army, going home
And once again, the pubs are stacked
And the discos, are full blown
Our wee town, is a nice wee town
But if you come to visit
Make sure you bring your umbrella
'Cause is always sure to drizzle.

Michael Singh

BALLYNAHONE - BALLYNAHONE

How dear you are to me,
For I am now in exile.
Across the stormy sea,
In nights' long dreams,
I often see the lights
that shine round home;
and all the friends I left behind,
in my lovely Ballynahone.

I can see the Moyola River,
as she gracefully flows along;
I can hear the wild birds singing,
that greet the early morn.
I can see the hills and valleys,
the paths that lead to home;
with rod and line, pastime I found,
round the hills of Ballynahone.

I still can see the turf fires burn,
as I did in days gone by;
when to the moss we cut turf,
and put them out to dry.
But to me, it is just a memory now,
and I'm so far from home;
but I'm sure the turf fires still burn bright,
in the homes of Ballynahone.

What would I give? I would give it all,
though rich that I may be;
to see again that lovely spot,
that's 'O' so dear to me.
And to walk again, that old bog road,
for it's there I often roamed.
To shake thehand of friendship,
with the folk round Ballynahone.

So fare-you-well, to foreign land,
with all your castles gay;
give to me that lovely spot
and the scent of new mown hay.
Far across the deep blue hills,
the hills that I call home;
God speed the day,
when I make my way,
to my lovely Ballynahone.

Thomas Hudson

MOMENTS CAPTURED UPON A STRAND

When the mist blows wildly through the air
And the wind blinds your eyes
When your hair beats wildly upon your face
And the sand beats a trail of madness
When the sky sings a sombre song of grey
And the sea rises to meet you
When the world turns darkly beautiful
And black is your favourite colour
When your throat jumps to meet the waves
And the cliffs impose on your solitude
When only the silence bides you joy
And night blends to a murky day
When your world is in a time of fantasy
And reality is of your making
When the clouds break with pouring lava
And your world is a time of stillness
In that moment is forever
And here you shall remain.

Dee Keys

Sweet Donegal

As gentle as a breeze
From the mountain and the sea
There's no place on God's earth
I would rather be
As a boy I longed for cities
Bright lights and liberty
But now I know in my heart and soul
There's only one place for me

And when I think of all those people
Rushing in city streets
I wonder where they're going
And whom they have to meet
The world has lots to offer
There are riches I am told
But I will choose my Donegal
For me it's my pot of gold

It's the quality of living
Not the quantity that counts
It's the friends you have and your family
You can't measure these amounts
It's your health, your smile, and your happiness
Peace of mind in great store
So much to be so thankful for
I couldn't want for more

For it's in the leaving that you learn
It makes coming home so sweet
The nod of the head, the wave of the hand
The 'oul' sod beneath my feet
There is beauty all around
So precious and so dear
Let's hear it for old Donegal
Let's sing and shout and cheer.

Damien McGrory

THE DERRY FOLK'S WEALTH

Only a dot on the geography scale,
As small as a minnow compared to a whale,
North, by north-west, of Ireland we go,
To find the historical Derry we know,

On the banks of the Foyle a great city rests,
The landscape divided from east bank to west,
But it is not only bridges which join us together,
It's the friendliest people in all types of weather,

How are ye doin' a greeting it sounds,
Between locals or to strangers who visit our town,
If you're lost, confused and out in the cold,
You'll get endless directions from the young or old,

The abundance of talent songwriters or singers,
Phil Coulter to Dana, including some swingers,
The literature of Seamus Heaney's aglow,
Of a genius inspired, we are proud of him so,

Famous people have come then gone,
Like President Clinton's American song,
His message of peace was welcomed by all,
As he spoke from a platform outside the Guildhall,

The Historical walls surrounding the city,
What now is our pride was once our pity,
The siege brought a famine to the people within,
The menu of rats, starvation the sin,

The warmth of the welcome within people's hearts
Is the added distinction which sets us apart,
The kindness the friendship are both in good health
These unequalled qualities of the Derry folk's wealth . . .

Martin Crawley

UNTITLED

Wherever I stand and look around
I fill with pride for my glorious town
Nip into the pub for the craic and the beer
There is no doubt, my heart lies here.
Surrounded by hills and fields of green
A more beautiful sight could ne'er be seen
Between the Donegal shores and the Antrim coast
It's a fabulous spot, but I needn't boast,
For the beauty and splendour speaks for itself
And the people contribute to its great wealth,
A friendlier bunch would never be found
In any city or any town
Sure it's a well-known fact never to query
The salt of the earth are bred here in Derry -
There's character etched in its historic face
There's a soothing air and a gentle grace.
I've lived here since the day of my birth
And Derry is the greatest town on earth.

Judith Taylor

ROSE OF THE SHIRES

Rose of the Shires,
Whose greener vales include the Nene
and whose once-remembered toils of skilful trade
remain long-gone.

Rose of the Shires
Those ancient stones remain to tell
of skirmish fought and distance won,
with clash of steel and rebel yell.

Rose of the Shires,
Whose own historic township shows,
in spreading wide the retail trade,
that money comes and prosperity grows.

Rose of the Shires,
Whose recent history celebrates
the work of one who's soon passed on
to peace, beyond the Althorp gate.

S Joyce

DOIRE . . .

Here in an old oak grove I lie,
Where I fell beneath an autumn sky.
Not spear nor sword had laid me low
But life itself ordained it so,
Long years ago when the earth was cold.

No children now above me play
Nor cattle homeward make their way.
No farmer toils, his crop to save
Where soft I sleep in winter grave,
But schemes of life, not death, unfold.

For soon the spring and you will see
The change that yet will come to me.
I'll raise my head from melted snow.
The acorn to an oak will grow.

Frank Donnelly

MY LITTLE VILLAGE ON THE FOYLE

At the mouth of the Foyle,
As you head out to sea,
There's a sweet little village
Where I long to be.
Its heart is the harbour
Where local men meet
Plotting and planning
The voyage for the fleet.
Its soul is the people
That live and work there,
Like Kealys, McLaughlin
Big Joe and Bovairds
Many miles I have travelled
Many more I will roam
But Greencastle's my anchor
The place I call home.

Trudy McLaughlin

CHAMELEON

Bisected by the River Foyle -
not far from Donegal -
a city full of 'villagers'
welcomes weary travellers
with open arms
and candid culture.

Flaunting siege walls and ancient soil,
boarding modern malls
where the latter day 'pillagers'
vie with canny cavillers
with all the charms
of feeding vultures.

No verse can capture
Derry's allure -
nor its peril.
It is home.

Pan Louis

MY NEIGHBOURS

I think they are a special race
They all seem very clever
Everyone keeps working on
No matter what the weather

They clean their windows
They clean their cars
They are always very busy
Everyone enjoys their life
No one's ever in a tissy

The children play
From dawn to dark
They get fun from simple pleasures
Like catching waspies in a jar
Or prancing in the heathers
The lawns are cut
The hedgerows trimmed
Everyone's place looks tidy
The kids are called
To go to bed
They all say nighty night.

Elizabeth Aulds

DERRY SWEET DERRY

Derry sweet Derry on the banks of the Foyle
Where I dream and I love
Where I sweat and I toil

Raging scenery and a history that's matching
A place of awe with an air that's catching
I'm part of it, I flow with it
I learn from it and I grow with it.

Derry sweet Derry on the banks of the Foyle
Where I dream and I love
Where I sweat and I toil

Steeped in music, laughter and song
Living here you can't go wrong
In a world that can be cold
Your people are warm
In a place that can be treacherous
You keep me from harm

Derry Sweet Derry on the banks of the Foyle
Where I dream and I love
Where I sweat and I toil.

J P McConnellogue

SPRING IN IRELAND

A golden freshness - spring is here.
As daffodils wave and ring good cheer.
The long clear evenings brighten up.
The Emerald Isle like a golden cup.

The snowy white lambs they skip and leap
The air is full of their gleeful bleat.
Through sun and shower - their carpet neat.
A field of green - a green serene.

The hedgerows burst into bud and leaf
The birds they twitter in loft and tree
The clouds are wafted far away
Spring in Ireland is a heavenly day.

Elizabeth M Jones

DAD'S ALLOTMENT

When I was a kid the family was poor
Working class, but proud were we
Hunger never knocked at our door
My dad rented an allotment you see

In the evenings after work his spade hit soil
He treasured his plot just like gold
Intricacies of plants him couldn't fail
As he would toil in the wet and cold

I saw leaves sprout all in a row
Potatoes down to radishes grew
Fruit trees' branches full would bow
The produce always looked so new

Tomatoes in the greenhouse bloomed
Other plants thrived under frame
This glory never seemed doomed
For this splendour dad was to blame

At home mum took over the glory
With jars to preserve and pans to cook
This is the start of another story
Meanwhile for an allotment I'll look

K J Humphrey

A DERRY VISION

Looking to a bright future
A toast with a bottle
Here's hoping and believing
Differing views, changing opinions
Us townsfolk seen it all
Lived through it, toughened so very tall

New opportunities to be grasped
Nations elite willing to invest
Never short of gratitude
It'll shorten the pitiful queue
Why the constant downbeat few

Reared in well-known places
For all the wrong reasons
Prejudice and judgement
No jury will overlook
This is my home!
Come and see the friendliness

Blackened tabloids, bad press
A community on the threshold
We'll take this chance
Why living in this twisted past
A land's majority will impress

Have I got it all down
Said too much
A penned onlooker upbeat
Never lost in a peaceful thought . . .

Seamus Murphy

PEACE AND PROSPERITY

Londonderry/Derry rises on the banks of the Foyle.
Its serenity belies its historical turmoil.
The Diamond, Shipquay Street and the Strand Road,
The ancient walls our ancestors bestowed.
The Creggan, Brandywell and the Bogside
Separated by the Foyle from the Waterside.
The imposing cathedrals of St Columb and St Eugene,
The stately Guildhall which completes the scene.
The ghosts of the past and the present weep,
As they wander disconsolately along night's empty streets.

That is the old city, but what of the new.
The Maiden has changed her whole point of view.
The Foyle Bridge imposing in its expansive structure,
Straddles the river in grandiose rapture.
Self-confident Foyleside aware of its splendour,
Disdainfully gazes at its humbler neighbours.
Quayside wearing a discontented frown
Having relinquished its place as the jewel in the crown.
The Craft Village precociously vying for attention.
The Richmond Centre, once a star, valiantly fights for redemption.

Supermarkets, leisure centres, cinemas with multi-screens,
Health farms, mystic retreats, parks so restful and serene.
Citizens have at last discovered a pride in their city,
After those dark years when all they felt was pity.
When the finest and the best were bombed to the ground
When the bang of explosions was a regular sound.
Anger and fear, discouragement and frustration;
The emotions felt at the futility of the situation.
Now there is a confidence about those in the street,
Happy and relaxed with a spring in their feet.

Angela Nutt

OF BALLYGAWLEYS' LAKE AND LAY-BY

Sun-drenched Sunday afternoon June 29
passes blissfully in a lay-by at Martray.
She was part of the old A4, running serpentine
which 30 years ago caused no delay.

Would the rushing weary traveller turn aside
for several moments as I have done.
Today the A4 is three lanes wide
and the speed of traffic visually stuns.

Spice Girls sing on car radios
while some drivers talk on mobile phones.
Some pull in and carelessly throw
the newly bought PC's box on the road.

For a moment I enjoy
the view from a picnic table.
A sheltered lay-by with nought to annoy
gives me chance to relax while I'm able.

Below in the valley, Martray Lake
peaceful and serene.
No turbulent ripple the waters make
though troubled times she sees.

The dwellers of the manor run Ardbeg Lodge;
the lovely brick building nearby,
Here one can savour an ample lunch
be it steak or an Ulster fry.

I awaken from my peaceful dreams
in my own garden on Cravenny Road.

Lloyd Noyes

JEWEL IN THE CROWN

Opportunity and privilege have been on my side,
And throughout this wonderful world I've travelled far and wide;
Yet wherever I wander, and no matter where I roam
Northern Ireland is the place I will always call my home.

And visitors to these shores most happily have found
The warmth of our welcome is justly renowned,
As too is our genial hospitality
And the magnificence of our diverse scenery.

For there is so much beauty whereof we can boast,
Like the glorious vistas all along the Antrim coast;
The majestic Mourne mountains, sweeping down to the sea;
And the Fermanagh Lakelands, with their great tranquillity.

From the bustling seaside towns of Bangor and Portrush,
To our castles, our gardens, parks and forests so lush;
From our nature reserves to stately houses' delights;
And from the Marble Arch Caves to our historic sites.

And our greatest claim to fame, the unique Giant's Causeway -
The giant, Finn McCool's cousin, for the legend does say
These hexagonal columns his fleeing feet created,
Leaving 'the eighth wonder of the world', as oft it is rated.

Yes, within the confines of our six small counties
Is a veritable banquet of rich scenic bounties;
And though the rain may appear all too regularly
We are yet blessed with a climate of rare extremity.

And, if a trip to Northern Ireland you're now contemplating
Come soon and discover all that here lies awaiting,
For the jewel in the crown of the Emerald Isle
Will make every visit most memorable and worthwhile.

Ian Caughey

THE WAY AHEAD

Oh River Foyle if you could only speak
What tales you could unfold
Of joyful days, of glory days
And things best left untold.
Now a Dutch king called Billy
And James who was a Scot,
For the crown of merry England
On Irish soil they fought.
And James lay siege to Derry
To conquer was his aim,
But up the Foyle came Billy
And put the Scot to shame.
So Derry was never taken
And a maiden still remains,
But I'm sure there's many who'll tell you
It's been taken again and again.
But let's put the past behind us
Let's trust in Him above,
He'll lead us through the storms of life
If we could only learn to love.

Michael J Downs

THE TROUBLES

When is it going to stop?
The killing and the grief.
Can't they see they're hurting people?
To them it's just another wreath.
Laid upon another grave,
Of another innocent soul.
Another family torn apart -
No longer whole.

They try to gain themselves respect and credibility.
They say they are fighting a war.
But normal, decent people are asking;
What is it all for?
Over the last two generations,
What have the troubles achieved?
Lining the politicians' pockets,
It's no comfort for the grieved.

Alisa McKee

I'M FROM NOTTINGHAM

On a bumpy, fetid and overcrowded bus
In Greece, on holiday,
A young man leaned towards me
I smiled back cautiously.
'You English?' he asked
I nod my head.
'Where abouts in England?'
'I'm from Nottingham' I say clearly.
'Nottingham, Nottingham' the word is echoed.
The crowd erupts in excitement
'Nottingham Forest'
'The European Cup'
'Super Reds'
'River Trent'
'Robin Hood'
'Brian Clough'
'Super Reds'
I smile and nod, basking in glory.
They think I'm special, just because
I'm from Nottingham.

E M Tomba

DAFFODILS AND WILLOW TREES

Swaying in the breeze of Spring
By a lake of shimmering hue,
Resplendent in your golden gowns,
Refreshed by morning dew,
Planted many years ago
To delight each generation,
Who muse beneath the willow trees
And watch Spring's revelation.

In a place of peace and solitude
Away from the city's roar,
And the never-ending traffic fumes
Which blacken every door,
Your golden frills hark back in time
To the days of youthful bliss,
As we stood beneath those willow trees
And shared a loving kiss.

(University Park Nottingham)

Joan Sabin

A WALK BY THE TRENT

i walked along by the water's edge
the warm sun shone brightly as i went
i saw nesting birds in the hawthorn hedge
as i strolled on the banks of the river trent

and i admired the river as it gently flows
and wends its way through wild countryside
and i see on calm river surface as it goes
the majestic white swans so serenely glide

i watch the rippling waters go travelling on
through wild meadows deep in lush green grass
then a field of colourful flowers i chanced upon
and smell their sweet scented fragrance as i pass

then i stop awhile and take a look around
at these breathtaking majestic sights i have seen
to admire these lovely wild jewels i have found
by the river trent with it lush meadows so green

A V Carlin

AS WE WERE - IN HEREFORD AND WORCESTER

Soon to be separated
Back to as we were
To our own boundaries
To our own identities.

We both have Cathedrals
To city status we're entitled
Both have rural communities
So there are similarities.

But some of us felt
- as counties go
We have been far too big
To operate successfully.

As for Worcester, we've already started
Committees are forming, coat-of-arms chosen
Let us hope, as forward we move
Each county will respond to the challenge ahead
For whatever the divide, of boundaries and councils
They will still be our neighbours
- the people of Hereford.

Mary A Slater

NOTTINGHAM!

Nottingham . . .
Our beloved city
Birthplace of Robin Hood -
Steeped in the history of his deeds
For the under-privileged.

His memory ever lingers
With the passing of the years -
His spirit lives among us
His strength allays our fears.

Hail! . . . Nottingham centenary
And Robin's merry men,
His leadership inspired them
Will Scarlet - Little John,
Friar Tuck and all the rest
They championed a cause . . .
Which still lives on
After many years
And everything's not lost.

Yes Nottingham . . . we're proud to be
Champions of your legendary
We hailed with joy
This year's centenary . . .
Long live Nottingham!

Mary Skelton

THE CITY OF NOTTINGHAM

In 1897 city status to Nottingham came
One hundred years later we celebrate same
Once a medieval town with people few
Over the years the population grew

Men were seen in bowler hats
Little girls with hair in plaits
Ladies demure in Victorian dress
Bathing costumes covered more not less

Horse-drawn carriages, trams on lines
The industrial era, men working down mines
Barges on canals plied their trade
1927, Council House foundations laid

Stalls once stood in the Old Market Square
Every year the traditional Goose Fair
Policemen with truncheons walked their beats
Trolley buses appeared on the streets

New buildings built by Fothergill and Hine
Railways arrived, canals in decline
Factories in the Lace Market produced fine lace
Progress in the city achieved rapid pace

Diesel buses now a familiar sight
Famous buildings floodlit by night
Queen of the Midlands Nottingham is renown
A modern city from that medieval town.

Brenda M Hadley

OLD NOTTINGHAM

The old Guardian office in its drab grey building
Folks hurrying to get their adverts in
Parliament Street with few cars and buses
Not any present day hurrying and rushes

The trolley buses ran down Carlton Road
If in no hurry the trolley poles would hold
But if you were rushed you could guarantee
Poles and wires would part and you'd be late for tea

The old central market with its front flower stalls
You could buy 12 chrysanths for five bob, no more,
behind them, cloth stalls, haberdashery and the life
I would cycle there, Saturdays, on my bike

Sneiton market was flanked by shops
with barrow boys shouting their wares
and an enormous lady, arms full of pots,
goading people to buy without cares

Drury Hill with its narrow, steep slope
Full of quaint shops, from where you could hope
to find anything unusual that you require
from copper brooches to all you desire.

I am Nottingham bred and born
and cannot help feeling a little forlorn
when I think of places no longer there
because of the planners' lack of care.

Perhaps in these enlightened times
we're a little more aware of the signs
and think before destroying all that's old
to leave only memories to unfold

Wendy Wild

STILL A QUIET PLACE

I remember visiting, as a child,
The Northern Cemetery, Bulwell, Nottingham.
Mother would take my small sister and me
Roughly once a fortnight,
And would lovingly tend her mother's grave.

We had a fair walk away from Bulwell's bustle.
En route, we saw a firm's buckets
Suspended from overhead lines, like crotchets on a stave.
We passed a huge, unsightly tip,
And, nearby, ate wild blackberries by the lane.

The quiet cemetery was usually bright with floral arrangements.
There was a dignified chapel with a spire,
And at least one green meadow.
In spring and summer we always needed to spot
Two or more hovering skylarks,
Overflowing with life and song,
High above the grounds.

In time, workers installed a new, shiny water tap,
But the water would suddenly gush out
And drench unwary feet!

Decades later, quarterly and unaccompanied,
I continue to visit the cemetery.
En route, only the blackberries, pleasingly, remain.

I check that three graves are tidy,
That the artificial flowers are creditable.

Although long deprived of its meadow and skylarks,
The cemetery now, in its well-tended parts,
Displays year-lasting and heart-warming colour.

And an energetic, shiny tap
Still drenches unwary feet!

Dora Hawkins

FLOWING MEMORIES

Years may come and years may go
But memories live forever.
I well recall, in days of yore,
The house where I was born,
And where my childhood days were spent
Beside the River Trent.

I knew that river's every mood,
Its every phase and flow.
On summer days, a gentle stream,
Its surface flecked with gold,
Swans with cygnets gliding by,
So peaceful and serene.
Some days a sheet of glittering stars
When stirred by gentle breeze,
But in the depths of winter's hold,
Black, and bleak, and cold,
When life upon its icy flow
Sought shelter in the rushes.
When storms beset, a raging mass
Of wind-tossed waves and currents,
Which sometimes made the surface seem
To switch its seaward stream.

Though years have flown, I still enjoy
A walk beside the river,
Enjoying every graceful sweep
Along its curving reaches,
And crystal clear those memories
Come flooding back to me,
Of happy days and sweet content,
Beside the River Trent.

Elizabeth Stokes

RECOLLECTIONS OF NOTTINGHAM

I recall the 'Daybrook Station'
The bridge across Mansfield Road.
Trains billowing steam o'er the rooftops
Trundling the lines with their load.

I remember the soldiers marching
Whistling a familiar refrain
My Mother tearfully calling,
'God Bless lads, come back again.'

The sound of their boots clung the road
As they marched out of sight
Carrying their heavy war load
Disappearing into the night.

I think of the many Christmases
Mam and Dad took us shopping in town
Being filled with delight, on seeing the tree
Bedecked in her glittering gown.

Seeing the Square, stilled, crisp and fresh
In her raiment of new fallen snow,
Clinging with glistening beauty
Capturing her soft afterglow.

In the quietness of my years
To my mind's eye, I frequently look
And privately shed a tear
As I open my memory book.

Recollections of life may be happy
Some may be sad
Recalling my past, here in, 'Nottingham'
Brings fond memories, of the life I have had.

Helen Laurel

SOUTHWELL MINSTER

With dog-toothed rounded arches
Of Britain's Norman days,
This house of prayer was started
By builders in this place.
As decades spread to centuries,
This parish church just grew,
Cathedral-like in splendour,
Such beauty there to view.
A Chapter House so wondrous
With countless carved stone leaves,
All history is here enshrined,
Beneath these sacred eaves.
A Roman tessellated floor;
A touch of Saxon art;
The skills of countless masons
Where each have played their part.
Our eyes roam round and upwards
From crypt to vaulted roof,
Herein lies England's history,
This is its living proof.

Within this quiet market town,
Where pilgrims' feet have trod,
Is one of England's treasures;
Southwell Minster, House of God.

John Sneath

THE ENIGMA OF ROBIN HOOD

Robin Hood, was he a fact,
Or a legend of the mind?
We scan all ancient records,
The truth therein to find.

Many are the claimants,
To dwell in Robin's fame,
But the local folk of Sherwood,
Cling firmly to his name.

Now hidden deep in fiction,
The numerous tales abound,
So our elusive hero,
Remains yet to be found.

The mighty oak of Edwinstowe,
Described as Robin's den,
Stands witness to the saga,
Of the outlaw and his men.

Tho' aged mists may mellow truth,
And warp the sense of time,
Many choose to wallow deep,
In rich historic rhyme.

So driven by the curious,
To dig, and sift and comb,
Perhaps a 'light' may yet emerge,
From some dark and dusty tome.

Yet in our minds he did exist,
And when all is said and done,
His name will last forever,
As Nottingham's famous son.

A A Walters

JEWEL OF THE MIDLANDS

Steeped in history, is Nottingham town
The jewel set in the Midland's crown,
From Wollaton Hall, to Castle Green,
Places of interest can be seen.

Atop the rock, The Castle grey,
Now houses art of yesterday.
Across the meadow can be found
Beside the Trent, the cricket ground.

On Castlegate stands Robin Hood,
'The Man In Green' of dale and wood.
Whose escapades, with merry band
Brought dubious fame through the land.

In Broadmarsh caves, beneath the floors,
Of Nottingham's most, prestigious stores
Tanners worked in days of yore
And locals sheltered from the war.

Card sharks met, Dick Turpin sold,
Ill-gotten gains in days of old.
And in their caverns, cool and deep
Olde Snottinghame lies fast asleep.

There's the Council house, fine market square,
The old Trip Inn, Ye Old Goose Fair.
So many facets has this city
No time to list all, more's the pity.

But if you like, enjoyment plus.
Be bold, be daring, visit us.

Hazel Vambria Walters

NOTTINGHAM

It's my city,
it's rushing, it's bustling
busy, busy
everyone on the move
on foot, on the bus in cars, lorries, vans
and the pavement sweeper
clears the pavement
of people
with its funny brushes
it gathers rubbish into its mouth
as it gobbles its way up Friar Lane
hoping one day to catch out
an unsuspecting traveller
waiting for a bus.

Along the same old Market Square a manky pigeon
toddles out from the crowd
under my feet.
I plan a poison-the-pigeons campaign.
Cruel?
Protect the pigeons?
What about the poor
unwanted and desperate
who also sleep on the city's roofs at night?
I often look up
haunted by this hidden need
in my city.
Who will love them
and beckon them down from their hiding places
in my city?

Yvonne Sewell

THE LONELY OLD MAN

Peace and solitude are all around,
with mist arising from the ground,
and up above the clouds so high
there is, I know, a clear blue sky.

Very soon gentle warmth will come,
with rays descending from the sun,
oh, if I could only stay,
in this woodland all the day.

Alas, I know I must go back,
to my cold and lonely shack,
to the place I've learnt to hate,
where poverty shares my cruel fate

A little longer, I will abide,
to see the beauty by my side,
a fir cone, a primrose or two,
and daisies peeping through the dew.

The hours are quickly passing now,
my body, no longer young somehow,
so, I must slowly wander down,
the country lane that leads to town.

When I get home, if one can so call,
I will remember, and enthral,
the lovely things nature provides,
then thank the Lord, that I have eyes.

Beryl Fidler

THE ILL-FITTING SHOES

We decided to go to Nottingham one day,
>we fancied a trip, so went on our way.
Walter I know was really hell-bent,
>on rowing a boat up and down River Trent.
So we went for a boat ride, then had a nice meal,
>then I noticed Walts' shoes were a bit down at heel.
We tried a few shops without much success,
>I said, 'You really must get some, they do look a mess.'
At last he did see some, made in Italy,
>they were shining bright, as smart as could be.
They were being wrapped up without further ado,
>but he said, 'I'll wear them now if it's alright with you?'
So he dumped his old shoes without any regret,
>I said, 'There are lots of places we've not been to yet.'
So we went up to the castle, then round Old Market Square,
>the winos and drop-outs were all gathered there.
So we thought it was time that we went for a drink,
>Where shall we go? Yates Wine Lodge I think.
From a big barrel we had a few doubles of wine,
>after all that, we felt really fine.
We met local people, had nice conversation,
>then it was time to make for the station.
I said, we must hurry to catch the next bus,
>I wondered why Walter was making a fuss.
He said, 'My feet hurt, I really can't walk very fast,'
Don't worry about buses, as long as we don't miss the last.
We arrived home at last, we'd had a good day,
>those Italian shoes came off straight away.
On picking them up, I did have to grin,
>as there was pieces of cardboard lining within.
With the cardboard out, they fitted a treat,
>then for comfort, those shoes, he found hard to beat.

Dorothy Mezaks

THE THREATENED ROSE

Rose of the Shires, how sweet your bloom,
you thorns take nothing from your charms.
Your beauty lies in valleys deep,
in summertime, in meadows sweet.
On rolling hills so gently curved
grow crops, graze sheep, quite undisturbed.

As summer cools to autumn time,
as fields lay bare and nights draw in.
As woodland canopy turns gold
and dormice nest beneath the leaves.
We walk, and see, and smell the change
that time inflicts upon the land.

The sunrise on a frosty morn
with all the countryside aglow.
A heron wings his way above,
his food source locked in ice below.
Our lakes and ponds in winter's grip
bear witness to our eastern link.

And so to spring the earth reborn,
a blackbird sings before the dawn.
The grass gleams with the morning dew,
and bluebells show their brilliant hue.
Four seasons now we've walked, and seen,
the pleasures that are here for free.

We must beware, for danger's near,
more homes and roads are built each year.
Mile by mile the urban sprawl
now threatens to devour it all.
Rose of the Shires, for whom we care
these thorns could pierce, beyond repair.

Juliette Blencowe

ROSE OF THE SHIRE

The grass is greener
Flowers bloom
Red rose glowing
When in full bloom.
Car racing, cricket, football too
Guy Fawkes plotted to blow up the Houses of Parliament
At Brixworth Manor House in the attic.
The civil war was at Brixworth too.
Charles I, was imprisoned at Holdenby Hall.
Brixworth Hall Park had prisoners in the war in the
Brixworth Hall. Italians, Germans all were there.
The stable to the hall still remains now called
The Lake House. Which is open to the public once a year.
Ducks and squirrels everywhere what a sight to see.
Birds singing, robins, blackbirds, martins, sing and coo.

Janet Childs

THE ROSE OF THE SHIRES

A picture postcard, could not do justice,
to the beauty that is you.
Your patchwork fields, your winding streams,
like threadwork bonding severed seams.

You offer historians, an interesting yield
with stately homes, and battlefields.
Your countryside walks, a rambler's delight.
Bringing ease to their knees, with no steep hill in sight.

Your rivers and lakes promise anglers good play,
and Wicksteed Park proves a great family day.
With your peaceful villages, boasting sleepy spires
you're my haven, my home, you're the 'Rose of the Shires'.

Lucy Drage

THE MONUMENT

By Severn's willow shaded banks, towers a monument strong and tall,
Her elegant spires pierce the skies, overseeing all.
Famed for the entombment of England's most infamous King,
A grey and sombre shroud for bishops, knights and their kin.

Steeped in past historic climes, those days long-gone before,
Compelling enthralled tourists to pause and gaze in awe.
Now silent after war-torn years, she stands magnificent and proud,
Sentinel to Worcester, faithful to Charles and Crown.

Witness to Cavaliers and Roundheads, fighting tooth and claw,
Subject to sacrilege and destruction of Cromwell's Civil War,
What scenes must those walls have witnessed in those disruptive times,
When Cromwell and Roundhead rang out from her
                                        their victorious chimes.

Now here within her precincts, with well-nurtured bordered lawns,
Sheltered from past winter winds, within ancient lichen covered walls,
'Tis here I've often wandered, North Porch through to Cloister,
The stained glass dedications compelling me to loiter.

Then overlooking the river, beyond the great West Door,
Here I've sat on wooden bench, next the boundary wall.
Often I did idle on a sultry summer's day,
Surveying weekend revellers, at leisure and at play.

Within the calm and quiet haze of these hallowed grounds,
There comes to me from far away those summer sights and sounds,
The prospect, on the river's bank of men intent on fishing,
The banter of young courting couples, romancing and kissing.

Keen anglers, they line the banks, contemplating floats,
Sounding their annoyance at would-be sailors mishandling their boats!
Through all I hear soft echoes of applause,
                                        enthusiasm for the Counties' cricket,
Most likely in praise of well-bowled ball or another fallen wicket!

An echo of spasmodic clapping carries across the water,
A steamer gently ripples by with revellers aboard her.
Upon all these things I reminisce and am thankful for the pleasure
Of salad days within ancient walls, pursuing weekend leisure.

William Holmes

REMEMBRANCE DAY IN WORCESTER

At eleven o'clock the city stopped,
motionless.
Shoppers looking back through tears
were turned to salt across the years,
seasoning the silent streets
with honour by their quietude.

Trapped in time, a truculent boy,
unnerved and overwhelmed by silence,
broke the ranks
to run a solitary gauntlet,
panicking to get away
from eyes that had survived, but now surveyed
his greenhorn progress past the endless line
of dumb commentators.

Then he became aware his nightmare
was only just beginning to unfold;
it prophesied a future running past
troops of ghostly quiet men
who paused for *him.*

Sheila Bath

THE FADING HEART OF WORCESTER

The city stands with cathedral so tall
Remnants apparent of fortress and wall
The boundaries crumbled and decayed
The magnificence gone since the first stone was laid

Beside the river, wearing mist-covered shroud
The past it beckons and shouts out aloud
Where have the streets and the timbered dwells gone
Today's new environment doesn't belong

The great river barges that once plied their trade
Are gone and forgotten, this travesty man-made
No more the activities, city-wide are they spread
The old times are forgotten, forgotten and dead

Like dreams of the night the river flows past
Taking with it, untold secrets, so fast
Planners today seem to do what they please
Destroying and building with malice and ease

Out of town complexes are springing like flowers
With non-sensical structures and hideous towers
The city is dying, the planners don't care
They're only just interested in their own fanfare

The shops are all closing, no one shares their plight
But promise does show, but it's only at night
Where taverns and clubs adorn the streets
And their bright coloured canopies flutter like sheets

To be proud of the city that's lost all its heart
We must really return and make a fresh start
Rebuild the city, the sights and the sound
Then again, we may have one, and be proud!

F L A Farmer

WITLEY COURT

Ancestral home
Burned-out shell

Exist
In my imaginings
Talk to me
Of ages past
of parasolled beauty
Transformed by time
The rape of your treasures
And the pain
Of disfiguration
Cry out
From the wilderness
Of your gardens
Statues gape lifelessly
From your fountains
And your pleasure domes
Have forgotten
The concept

What shadows moved amongst the topiary
Oh Rachel Anne!
When you bathed that day?

The Earl sold out
In grief and debt
To the highest bidder

We have learned by fire the danger of complacency
We smile warily amidst your ruins
We are the uninvited
And we walk uneasily
Through the graveyard of our own dreams

Rose Marshall

TIME

Through towns and cities,
   The Severn river flows,
Past meadows where buttercups and
                          willows grow,
Swifts soar and dive by its shores below.

Fishermen on a misty river start a match,
But sneaky heron sees his chance and
Steals someone else's catch.

Worcester's old cathedral seen it all
   People, fashion, and civil war.
Majestic swans glide by
A lonely seagull cries.
Time has come,
And time has gone,
But the Severn river
Keeps moving on.

Sandra Wood

HOME

Home is where the heart is, but where is that to me?
For in my soul I have not one, but a very special three.
My heart is in my homeland where I grew up so fast,
Those green and pleasant islands, my home now in the past.
And also with my parents, now settled somewhere new
My home is where I'm always loved so special and so true.
My home is with my true love, wherever that may be
For I will have my home with him, as he will have with me.
Home is where the heart is, this I do now know -
It's where I am most happy, and always will be so.

Tanya Jane Corsie

THE OIL CITY

This grey granite town
Sparkles in the sun
Shivers in the moonlight
Another day is done

In past times known for fishing
Where lives were lost to slave and toil
There would be a saviour to our labours
It's a wondrous thing this word oil.

It started off quite slowly
Then it turned life on its head
Just ask any Aberdonian
If they know the price of bread.

Twenty years have past
You wouldn't know the place
Buildings spring up from nowhere
Of the fishing boats
There's hardly any trace.

This oil will not last
As we dread the day it's through
To find a job without it's hard
Though scores of people will have to.

Heading towards the millennium
You wonder what's in store
For the city of Aberdeen
Be it boom-time or a fall.

Graham Davidson

SOCIAL FLOW

At last these working fires fade,
And craftsmen slowly leave their trade
In mourning for what they once made,
        and thought instead.
Anti-social minds put paid
        to what's now dead.

Providing seas with steel-hulled boats
Initiated 'Red Clyde' votes,
And slaked reactionary throats.
        No thought in-bred.
Empty docks where nothing floats
        except what's dead.

Monumental cranes now stand,
An idle, rusting, vacant band,
Gibbet like, now second-hand.
        The thought has sped.
Silence settles where all the sand
        conceals what's dead.

A prestige, garden-walled estate
Lies smug behind the shipyard gate.
A union in which none relate
        with thought, but dread
What maritime momentoes wait
        among what's dead.

Commercial captains steer their way
Between the banks of what they say
Now is the river of the day,
        and thought they led
The fleet. But sunken eyes betray
        those times are dead.

J Hunter

HOME

City of rock,
Sits proud in the north.
Shimmering silver,
That lights up the sea.

City of green,
So hard to let go.
The honey of hillsides,
With roots taken hold.

City of lights,
Shine up in the dark.
Flashes of gold,
That welcome you home.

City of birth,
In my heart I'll keep.
The rush of the rivers,
That hush you to sleep.

Sally Joanne Bell

INFORMATION

We hope you have enjoyed reading this book - and that you will continue to enjoy it in the coming years.

If you like reading and writing poetry drop us a line, or give us a call, and we'll send you a free information pack.

Write to :-
Anchor Books Information
1-2 Wainman Road
Woodston
Peterborough
PE2 7BU
(01733) 230761